A Multicultural Guide to
Thematic Units
for Young Children

by
Dr. Jeri A. Carroll
and
Dr. Dennis J. Kear

with an introduction by
Tonya Huber

illustrated by Darcy Tom

Cover by Darcy Tom

Good Apple
1204 Buchanan St., Box 299
Carthage, IL 62321-0299

S I M O N & S C H U S T E R *A Paramount Communications Company*

Copyright © 1993, Good Apple

ISBN No. 0-86653-715-5

Printing No. 987654321

Good Apple
1204 Buchanan St., Box 299
Carthage, IL 62321-0299

Preface

The writing of this book was an adventure in and of itself. Much time was spent in the libraries, in community centers, talking with people from a variety of backgrounds, observing various shows, listening to radio talk shows, looking at early childhood materials, and talking with early childhood teachers. We learned as we wrote, and we continue to respond to those around us with our new-found information. In this way, the writing of this book is never over.

The contributions of each of the cultural groups is unknown to so many of us. Tracing peanuts from Central and South America to Spain to Africa and back to the Americas shows how strongly each cultural group influenced the production and eating of peanuts here today. And yet, we so seldom mention these contributions when we teach.

It is our hope that this book gives some of that information to teachers who can share it with their children who will grow in their understanding and acceptance of others. In this way learning to understand and accept others is never over.

GA1432

Table of Contents

GA1432

Introduction
by
Tonya Huber, Ph.D.

America is home for two thirds of the world's immigrants (Hodgkinson, 1990). It stands as the most diverse nation of peoples, languages, cultures and customs in the world. Small wonder, then, that America's educators are currently facing some of the most demanding dilemmas in the history of education. What does *diversity* mean to the classroom teacher? How does a teacher teach *about* diversity? How does a teacher teach *to* diversity? These resources and activities include options that are inclusive of the diverse heritages of peoples who collectively make up the nation known as "America." The appreciation of traditions, history, and customs help us understand similar cross-cultural experiences that unite all people.

Native American Peoples

American Indians, the Native American peoples, are the smallest of the American ethnic minority groups in population, yet represent the greatest diversity. According to 1990 census data (Hodgkinson, 1990), the 1.7 million American Indians make up only 1 percent of the nation's population while accounting for as much of the diversity as the other 99 percent combined (p. 1). Of some 2000 language groupings in the 1490's, at least 200 (according to some sources as many as 300) native languages are still spoken today. These languages present the stories of more than 400 tribes and nations of Native Americans and Alaskan Native peoples.

Peoples of Hispanic Heritage

Hispanic peoples are the largest growing American ethnic minority group. Hispanic subgroups include Mexican Americans, Puerto Ricans, Cubans, Central and South Americans, and other peoples of Spanish heritage. The first European settlers within what we now know as the continental United States were Spanish who established the Spanish-speaking communities that would become Sante Fe, New Mexico, and St. Augustine, Florida, before Columbus landed at Hispaniola, before the English settlements at Sagadahoc and Plymouth Colony established by the Pilgrims.

Mexican Americans are the largest subgroup and historically and culturally bonded to the Native American peoples. Many creation stories remind us that the geographical divisions separating the continent of North America are man-made. As such, they are artificial divisions that separate peoples and lands once intimately connected. These peoples represent the indigenous peoples of North America. Treaties, land cessions, and wars have aided in the division of

GA1432

the land and the people. Though differences and divisions exist, the stories and traditions remind us that all people are related, "mitakuye oyasin" in the Lakota tribal language.

Peoples of European Heritage

Americans of European heritage make up the "macroculture," or majority group, in the United States. Varied regions and different countries provide a rich diversity of languages, heroes, traditions and customs from countries as different as Britain, Germany, Poland, France, Ireland, and Russia. As these immigrants claimed regions of the North American continent for their new homelands, the regional distinctions including midwest, south, southwest, northwest, east became known. Colonization and statehood defined new divisions: Pennsylvania, Virginia, Massachusetts, Florida, Kansas, Kentucky, Oklahoma, New Mexico, Alaska and Hawaii–eventually fifty states in all.

Peoples of African Heritage

Just as the story of this country's expansion includes the displacement of the Native American and Mexican peoples from their traditional homelands, so does it include the story of African peoples who were forced from their homelands to this country to serve as slave labor.

Black Americans, often inappropriately grouped together as "African Americans," are peoples initially drawn from a diverse range of cultures and countries in Africa, and later from the Caribbean, Central and South America. Black Americans represent the largest minority group in America. Because of the great diversity in the peoples known as Black Americans, their stories come from all over the world.

Peoples of Asian Heritage

The newest arrivals to the American mosaic are the peoples of Asian and Pacific Islander heritage. While initial immigration to the North American continent from China occurred in 499, major immigration of Chinese and Filipino peoples would not occur until the 1760's and late 1700's, with Japanese and Korean peoples immigrating in the mid to late 1800's. More recently, Vietnamese, Cambodian, Hmong, Laotian and other Asian and Pacific Islander peoples have added to the rich traditions celebrated in America.

GA1432

Many Backgrounds

While the activities and experiences included in this book are intended to be responsive to diverse cultures, they are in no way intended to be a comprehensive representation of the multitude of peoples enjoying American nationality. Rather, the experiences included in this collection were each developed with options to explore the richness of diverse heritages. The activities present multiple perspectives and, as such, step beyond the first step of multicultural education, multicultural content. The diversity of the nation's classrooms demands a sensitivity to and respect for cultural differences.

These activities have been developed as springboards for teachers to launch children on exciting voyages of learning. But, perhaps more importantly, these activities highlight the need for understanding where we have been as a people, where we are as a nation, and where we may yet journey as a multiculturally diverse mosaic of peoples.

Since research reports that teachers build upwards of 65 percent of classroom time around printed instructional materials, educators need to think critically about the quality of material that impacts so significantly on the learners' time. This requires awareness on the part of the teacher of her own ethnic growth and multicultural understanding.

Boyer (1990) has identified eight stages of ethnic growth, reminding educators that cultural, racial, social, and related factors associated with human development cannot be ignored.

> All socialization emerges from the totality of one's experiences, and those experiences take place in an environment communicating many messages. Such messages are central to the value placed on one's ethnic identity. In other words, one looks for reflections of one's family, race, language, religion, music, recreative practices, and art. Further, such expectations, when not met, deliver a powerful message of rejection, illegitimacy, and questionable academic involvement to the learner. (p. 35)

Boyer goes on to remind educators that

> a psychosocial instructional connectedness occurs within learners when they subconsciously identify with, or relate to, the human profile or human event which constitutes the required content for study in school. This includes (1) the nature of the story, (2) the conclusions drawn from direct storytelling, and (3) the indirect messages delivered as a result of story lines. (p. 35)

GA1432

Because of the strong connection between ethnic growth and academic achievement, the states of ethnic growth should be considered by teachers from a personal perspective and then from a professional perspective as they select curriculum and instruction. Boyer posits we move from nonexistence in curriculum through states of existence, tolerance, recognition, acceptance, respect, appreciation, and, finally, celebration. (For explanation of these states, see Boyer, 1990, p. 1.)

Students need skillful and knowledgeable teachers to open for them the door to diversity beyond which is found a rich and complex global people bonded by similar experiences, feelings, fears and loves. It is a diversity made of many people sharing one world.

Related Readings

Boyer, J.B. (1990). *Curriculum Materials for Ethnic Diversity*. Lawrence, KS: Center for Black Leadership.

Hodgkinson, H.L. (1990). *The Demographics of American Indians: One Percent of the People; Fifty Percent of the Diversity*. Washington, D.C.: Institute for Educational Leadership/Center for Demographic Policy.

Huber, T., and Pewewardy, C.D. (in press). *Culturally Responsible Pedagogy: Knowledge Base, Application, and Practice*. Bloomington, IN: National Educational Service.

National Education Association. (1987, June) *. . . And Justice for All*. Washington, D.C.: National Education Association Study Group Reports on Ethnic Minority Concerns.

National Institute of Education. (1980). *Students' Knowledge of Textbook Content*. Washington, D.C.: Department of Education.

Quality Education for Minorities Project. (1990). *Education That Works: An Action Plan for the Education of Minorities*. Cambridge, MA: Massachusetts Institute of Technology.

GA1432

About This Book

A Multicultural Guide to Thematic Units for Young Children is meant to be a companion to *A Multicultural Guide to Literature-Based Whole Language Activities* which provides activities based on a book/story that the teacher reads/tells to the children. *A Multicultural Guide to Thematic Units for Young Children* provides a multicultural perspective to several units of study for young children.

The units in this book are chosen because of their interest to young children, and the experiences and activities described can therefore be meaningful. Most of the units are based in the social studies or in the sciences. We have approached those in the social studies from an expanding horizons perspective.

> "As we look at goals that are typically set for young children in social studies, we find ones that start with self, expand through family, friends, schools, communities, cities, states, countries, etc. However, a closer examination of the curricula would suggest that we also present materials on human dignity, respect for human life, an appreciation for the rights of others, survival, interdependence, economy, making choices, ethnicity, relating to others, and the uniqueness of individuals." (Wells, C.B., and Carroll, J.A. (1986). *Famous Friends: Pathfinders*. Carthage, IL; Good Apple, Inc.).

Each social studies unit starts with something that is familiar to the child (his/her own family), asks him to look at the families of those he knows best (his friends or classmates), and allows him to examine the family structure of others (through the listing of multicultural books at the end of each unit). In this examination children are encouraged to look at the similarities and differences in an accepting manner.

Each science unit starts with information about how and why the unit might be considered in a multicultural study. Just where did peanuts come from? South America? Did the Spanish explorers take them back to Europe? Did the Spanish then take them to Africa? Did the Africans brought here to be slaves bring them on the ships with them? And how many ways did George Washington Carver discover to use them? Do we all eat them? A list of multicultural children's books appears at the end of each unit. Background information was taken from the following three sources:

The New Book of Knowledge. (1987). Danbury, CT: Grolier, Inc.

Compton's Encyclopedia. (1985). Chicago: Division of Encyclopedia Britannica, Inc.

The World Book Encyclopedia. (1990). Chicago: World Book, Inc.

GA1432

Take-Home Books

Because we know that parents are key participants in each child's education, each unit has a take-home sheet which can be made into a book or used as a work sheet which reviews what the children have learned about the topic. Teachers are encouraged to review it with the children, allow the children to work together in groups to complete it, and talk about it as they work. Just before they go home, again review it with them and encourage them to tell their parents all about what they learned in school that day or week.

Different People Do Things Different Ways

In addition to the take-home book/sheet, there is a picture frame made up of many children of many races/cultural groups. At the top of the frame is a sentence telling about the theme and how it relates to many different peoples. Children are encouraged to draw pictures showing their new-found knowledge.

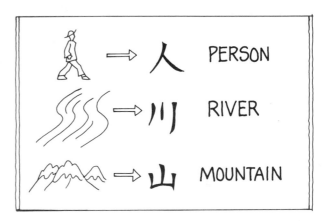

Different people use different alphabets.

Multicultural Education

We have purposefully not given a simple definition of multicultural education. Our fear was that with a simple definition, we would lead teachers to think they understood the intricacies of the various racial and cultural groups, which can never be. We have provided opportunities for adults and children alike to expand their views and acceptances of the various groups of people through the processes of comparing and contrasting. When the trip through these activities is finished, everyone's awareness will have been heightened and hopefully everyone will want to find out more.

Developmentally Appropriate Programs

As with all programs for young children, remember that the majority of the time spent with young children ought to be spent by the children investigating and exploring meaningful materials and ideas in a natural way. Some of the activities are for the whole group at circle time. Some allow you to work with individuals or small groups. Children must be allowed to talk with each other and adults about the information they are learning. They must investigate with their whole beings. They are concrete learners. They need to explore.

GA1432

Alphabet

The alphabet is a group of signs used to write a language. These signs called letters express all the sounds that people make when they speak. The letters are put together to make words.

For the most part we learn to recite the alphabet letters in order. That does not mean that we learn them in order or that they evolved in that order. In fact, if we mixed up the order, it would make no difference. The letters are still there. Some reading systems require that the children learn them in the frontwards order and in the backwards order. It makes no difference. Children are most likely to learn letters first that are consistently in their personal environment, which includes their written name, television station call letters, cereal boxes and fast-food signs.

Our alphabet has its roots in the Roman and Latin alphabets which had been modified from the Greek which came from the Semitic writing system. Almost all alphabets except the Korean one come from the Semitic writing system. Interestingly enough, in the early alphabets many of the letters were printed backwards.

The alphabet name comes from the first two letters of the Greek alphabet, *alpha* and *beta*. Capital and small letters are a relatively new innovation coming from the Middle Ages. Printing was used for official documents and monuments while cursive was used only on less official documents like letters.

Alphabet Soup

Buy dried alphabet noodles. Boil them, run cold water over them and give each child a group of noodles. Ask them to find all the letters of the alphabet. When they have all of the letters, allow them to place them in a cup of broth and eat the alphabet.

GA1432

What Does This Say?

Give children alphabet noodles. Have them write words on one half of a word card with the noodles and illustrate the word on the other half. Older children can write sentences to their friends.

Send messages home to parents about the study of the alphabet by having the children glue the letters to a black piece of paper.

They All Start with the Same Letter

Some of the alphabet books have more than one word that starts with any one letter. Older children can make alphabet books where the word and illustration become a simple three-word phrase or sentence: Aunt Annie's alligator, big blue bug, Christmas candy cane, etc.

ABC Order

Have the children take time to alphabetize things that they are familiar with. Alphabet cards and word cards help at the beginning. Have the children place the alphabet letters in order by looking at the one posted in the room. When that is done, have them put the words next to the alphabet letters and then copy them onto paper in order.

Try several different things: first names, last names, moms' names, dads' names, animals, birds, cars, parts of a car, businesses, television celebrities, cartoon characters, etc.

Some Alphabets Are Different

Examine the alphabets of the different languages. Many of these are available in the encyclopedias that we mentioned in the introduction. One is below.

АБВГДЕЁЖЗИЙКЛМНОП
РСТУФХЦЧШЩЪЫЬЭЮЯ

The Russian alphabet, properly called the Cyrillic alphabet, has 33 characters.

Read the story *Here Comes the Cat* and have the children find the letters from above in the phrase "here comes the cat."

Making the Alphabet

Let children make the alphabet letters in many different ways. Try . . .

glue and glitter

sandpaper

playdough

cookie dough

watercolors

tempera

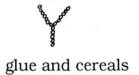
glue and cereals

stencil tracing

glue and colored sand

mud and let it dry

glue and rice

glue and corn

ABCDEFGHIJKLMNOPQRSTUVWXYZ

GA1432

Alphabet Books

Choose a topic for an alphabet book–Home A to Z, School A to Z, Our Town A to Z, etc. Give each child one letter of the alphabet to illustrate. He must think of something at home, school or in town to illustrate something that starts with that letter. Choose a way to put the letter on the paper from the activities listed above.

After a thorough study of the various cultures, have children make a multicultural alphabet book where they have to come up with words from the various cultures, not one word per culture per page, but a smattering of the cultures throughout the pages.

Handmade Letters

The book *The Handmade Alphabet* shows the manual alphabet of The American Sign Language. Children learn these formations quickly.

Learn to spell names.
Sign to the children to sit.
Call roll in sign.
Line up by sign.

N A M E

Put Them in Order

Give each child a piece of adding machine tape that is at least 26" (66.04 cm) long. Run off copies of the alphabet letters in 1" (2.54 cm) grids. Have the children cut out the alphabet letters and glue them in order onto the adding machine tape. When ready, children can draw a small picture next to each letter that begins with that letter.

Letters in the News

Give each child a piece of a newspaper and have him find each of the letters in the alphabet. Glue them into boxes on 1" (2.54 cm) grid paper.

When ready, children can cut out whole words, one beginning with each letter, and glue them onto adding machine tape in order.

Children's Books

Agard, J. (1989). *The Calypso Alphabet.* New York: Henry Holt and Company.

Vagin, V., and Asch, F. (1989). *Here Comes the Cat.* New York: Scholastic, Inc.

Feelings, M. (1974). *Jambo Means Hello: Swahili Alphabet Book.* New York: Dial.

Isadora, R. (1983). *City Seen from A to Z.* New York: Greenwillow Books.

Musgrove, M. (1976). *Ashanti to Zulu: African Traditions.* New York: Dial Books.

Rankin, L. (1991). *The Handmade Alphabet.* New York: Dial Books.

GA1432

Alphabet Take-Home Book

Read the story. Draw the pictures. Cut out the boxes. Put the pictures in order. Staple them together. Make a cover. Read the story to a friend. Take it home. Read it to someone at home.

I can write these letters.

These letters are in my name.

These are my favorite letters.

These letters are hard to write.

I write these words with letters.

These letters are mixed up.

Different people use different alphabets.

6

Birthdays

Birthdays are special holidays. Before the calendar was invented, birthdays were not celebrated because we had no way of numbering the days. Everyone knew that people grew older as time passed, but they had no way of marking the milestone. After the calendar was invented, we were able to number the days in a year and anniversaries became important. Special celebrations grew up around birthdays.

It is thought that ancient Egyptians were the first to honor birthdays with celebrations. For many years only the birthdays of important men or ancestors were celebrated. The Germans are given credit for starting celebrations of children's birthdays. Parties, presents, cakes, candles, games, and good wishes have long been part of birthday celebrations. In some countries, it is a tradition to plant a tree on the day a baby is born to bring him or her good luck during his or her lifetime.

When Is Your Birthday?

Give each child a strip of paper and have him record when his birthday is on that strip. (If the child is too young to do so, do it for him.)

Place twelve pieces of paper on the floor. Label each one with one month of the year. Have children find their months and place their birthday strips on the paper. Once all strips are on the paper, have the children put the strips in numerical order. Glue them onto the paper.

Record the number in each month on a graph. Post the pieces of paper in the room. Check off the birthdays as you celebrate them. (Note, we did not say as they happen. This would eliminate the summer birthday children.)

Birthday Celebrations

Set up a way to celebrate each child's birthday in your classroom. In some areas, parents will provide the party and the treats. In other areas, parents cannot. In those areas if you choose to celebrate with a cake, ask the parents to send a cake mix and icing and bake the cake on site. If they do not, have one on hand. Set aside twenty minutes to bake the cake, with the birthday child "in charge," and another ten minutes to eat it. Baking is a great cooperative learning science activity. Eating is a great social activity.

GA1432

Summer Birthdays

Be sure to celebrate the birthdays of the children who have them in the summer. There are several times to celebrate them.

Unbirthdays

If you have posted the birthdays for the twelve months as suggested in the first activity, choose months that have few birthdays and ask the summer birthday children to celebrate during that month.

Half Birthdays

Have the children count six months from their birthdays and celebrate their half birthdays rather than their birthdays.

By the Month

Celebrate the birthdays by the month at the end of each month. In September celebrate all summer and September birthdays. That way, summer birthdays get to come first instead of last.

Birthday Cards

Make a birthday card box that contains materials to make birthday cards. Children can use the box when they want to make cards to take to parents, send to grandparents or other relatives.

Include in the box card stock paper folded in half, envelopes to fit the card, crayons, markers, felt tip pens, construction paper, glue, sample birthday cards, word cards with simple messages on them. Replenish periodically.

When I'm Older

Children seem to always want to do everything that the big kids do. Let them realize that they can do certain things now and that they will probably be able to do certain things later.

Give each child a large piece of paper folded into thirds. On one of the thirds glue a picture of a baby. On one of the thirds glue a picture of a child. On one of the thirds glue a picture of a teenager or adult.

In each of the thirds have the children draw or glue pictures of things that they did, can do, or will do at the different life stages. Items might include toys, clothes, or activities.

GA1432

A Birthday Gift for My Mom/Dad

Many times young children would like to give their parents something, but most often what they want to give them is something that they themselves want. In order to help the process of learning to think about what others want, have the children try to think of and record a gift that they would like to give their parents.

Give each child a piece of paper, glue, magazines, pencils, markers, scissors. On the piece of paper have him draw a picture of his mom or dad and write "Just for Dad" or "Just for Mom" at the top. Sort through the magazines and cut out pictures of things that he would like to buy for that person and glue them onto the piece of paper.

Provide pieces of construction paper of various sizes in the shape of boxes. Children need to try the size of box to cover the picture and then decorate the boxes with ribbon and glitter. Glue the boxes over the pictures of the things that they have drawn for their moms and/or dads. Glue the box just at the top of the picture so the box can be lifted up and the gift can only then be seen.

Children's Books

Adoff, A. (1991). *Hard to Be Six.* New York: Lothrop, Lee & Shepard Books.

Bannon, L. (1939). *Manuela's Birthday.* Chicago: Albert Whitman & Company.

Bannon, L. (1961). *The Gift of Hawaii.* Chicago: Albert Whitman & Company.

Clifton, L. (1973). *Don't You Remember?* New York: E.P. Dutton & Co., Inc.

Fleischman, P. (1979). *The Birthday Tree.* New York: Harper & Row Publishers.

Hertz, O. (1981). *Tobias Has a Birthday.* Minneapolis, MN: Carolrhoda Books, Inc.

Johnson, L.S. (1963). *Happy Birthdays Around the World.* Chicago: Rand McNally and Company.

Keats, E. (1968). *A Letter to Amy.* New York: Harper & Row Publishers.

Patterson, L. (1965). *A Holiday Book: Birthdays.* Champaign, IL: Garrard Publishing Company.

Politi, L. (1948). *Juanita.* New York: Charles Scribner's Sons.

Rylant, C. (1987). *Birthday Presents.* New York: Orchard Books.

Uchida, Y. (1966). *Sumi's Special Happening.* New York: Charles Scribner's Sons.

All About Me Cake

Put the right number of candles on the cake to show how old you are. On each candle write something that describes you. Color the cake.

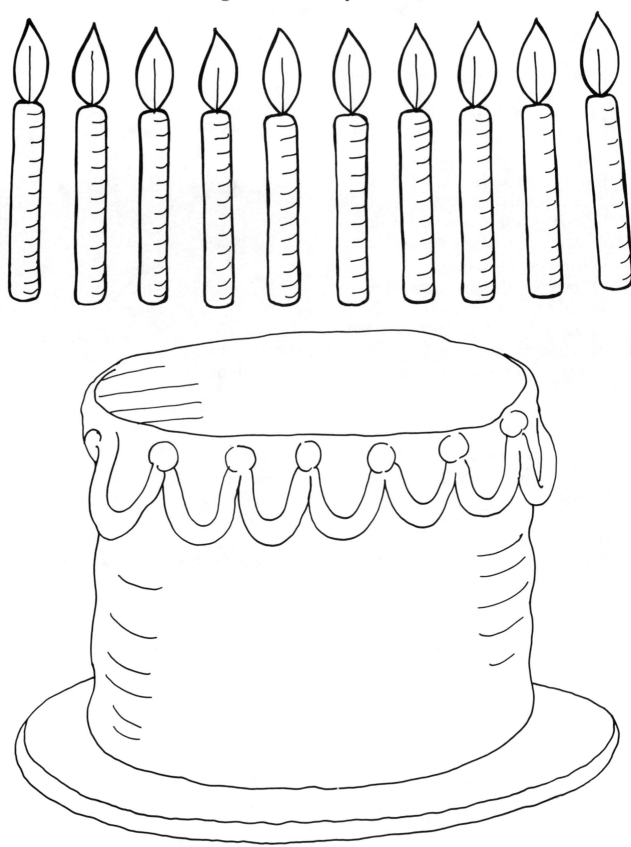

10

Birthdays Take-Home Book

Read the story. Draw the pictures. Cut out the boxes. Put the pictures in order. Staple them together. Make a cover. Read the story to a friend. Take it home. Read it to someone at home.

This is me on my birthday.

This is my mom on her birthday.

This is my dad on his birthday.

Guess whose birthday this is.

This is my friend's birthday.

This is my teacher's birthday.

All people have birthdays.

12

Celebrations

Celebrations

Celebrations come in all varieties. They are solemn, joyous, repentent, or honoring. Most celebrations occur once a year and may last for as long as a day or a year. Some honor great leaders, saints, gods, or spirits. Others celebrate a harvest, beginning of a season or year, or the anniversary of an historical event. From the variety of celebrations, it is evident that although most are joyous occasions, some involve mourning and repentance.

In order to show that a celebration is occurring, people don decorations of many kinds. They might decorate their houses and streets. They might wear special clothing. Some exchange gifts. Others celebrate with special meals, dancing and/or parades. Most solemn celebrations do not use these festive activities to "celebrate." These celebrations are observed with fasts, meditation and prayer.

In the past most feasts and festivals were religious. However, today many feasts and festivals celebrate nonreligious events.

What Do *You* Celebrate?

Celebrations are when we spend focused time thinking about thanking, honoring, remembering. Different celebrations are celebrated different ways. Different cultures celebrate different events in different ways.

Brainstorm with the children the different times of celebration that they can think of. List these on chart paper.

Choose one to discuss daily for a week. During the discussions, let the children tell you ways their family celebrates that particular event.

Fireworks

Fireworks are used in various cultures for different celebrations. Fireworks are used to celebrate the new year, football games, Independence Day, festivals, and Christmas.

Let children make fireworks pictures with red, blue, white and green paint and black paper.

Put the black paper on newspaper on the floor. Place the paint on the table in shallow containers. Have children load their brushes with paint and splash/drop it onto their papers.

When the pictures are done, have them write the day that is being celebrated on the pictures. Do this after reading several of the books at the end of this unit. Children will then have their own experience and some newly acquired knowledge about celebrations.

by Sharon SpeKaes

What's Happening?

Be sure to take part in the cultural events in your community. Your children will love seeing you there. It will also be important to the parents.

Cakewalk

Today cakewalks are usually held at fund-raising events. Children will have fun getting their snacks using a cakewalk format. Place numbers or letters on the floor and the same numbers or letters in a jar. Have each child stand on a number to start. Play music. When the music stops, they must stand on a letter or number. Draw a letter or number out of a jar. That child gets his/her snack. In order to speed up things, pick out three to four numbers/letters at a time.

You Are Special

Children do many special things during their time in school that parents never know about. Use the ditto at the end of this unit to send home when this happens. The writing space is large enough to allow you to put a photograph of the child doing that something special. It would be even more special to have the children cut out the circle and mount the entire message on construction paper.

Crowns for the Celebrating

Whenever you celebrate, crowns are fun. A special one can be made by the class for use on birthdays. For other occasions, let each child make one.

Select a color of bulletin board edging. Cut a strip the size of each child's head plus 1"-2" (2.54-5.08 cm) of overlap for stapling.

While the strips are still flat, have the children glue on sequins, "jewels" and glitter. Let them dry before stapling or else you will end up with glue in the hair.

When Shall We Celebrate

Most often we celebrate and investigate different things according to a calendar. We examine the different cultures only at specific times. In order to avoid that, celebrate Martin Luther King in September (citizenship time, not his birthday) and celebrate the Native Americans in the spring (care of the earth, not Thanksgiving).

Celebrations Take-Home Books

Use the ditto at the end of this unit for the children to take home to read to their parents. Give them extra pieces of paper to make additional pages if they choose. When they have finished and before they take the books home, have them read them to a partner.

15

Foods for Celebrations

From the list of celebrations that children generated, choose five. Write the name of the celebration at the top of a large piece of paper. Divide your class into five groups. Give each group one piece of paper with a celebration noted at the top.

Provide magazines, scissors, glue, crayons. The task is to cut out foods that are typical foods for the celebrations that they have been assigned. If they cannot find foods, they can draw/color them onto their paper.

Who Celebrates What When?

Advanced first and second graders can try this. Choose one holiday to investigate (New Year's or Independence Day are good ones). Have children try to find out when as many different cultures and countries celebrate the holiday as possible. List the holiday and the date on a sheet of paper. Put them in chronological order and post in the room.

For information when festival days are, purchase a Cultural and Festival Days of the World poster from the Educational Extension Systems, P.O. Box 259, Clarks Summit, PA 18411 (1-800-447-8561).

Children's Books

Bonnici, P. (1985). *The Festival.* Minneapolis: Carolrhoda Books, Inc.

Balet, J. (1969). *The Fence.* New York: Seymour Lawrence Delacorte Press.

Gramatky, H. (1961). *Bolivar.* New York: G.P. Putnam's Sons.

Howe, J., and Blake, M. (1991). *Dances with Wolves: A Story for Children.* New York: Newmarket Press.

Leaf, M. (1936, 1964). *Ferdinand.* New York: Viking Press, Inc.

Margolies, B.A. (1990). *Rehema's Journey: A Visit in Tanzania.* New York: Scholastic, Inc.

McKissack, P.C. (1988). *Mirandy and Brother Wind.* New York: Alfred A. Knopf.

You Are Special

Draw a picture to show some way you are special.

17

Celebrations Take-Home Book

Read the story. Color the pictures. Cut out the boxes. Put the pictures in order. Staple them together. Make a cover. Read the story to a friend. Take it home. Read it to someone at home.

We celebrate birthdays.

We celebrate the new year.

We celebrate the harvest.

We celebrate with fireworks.

We celebrate with people.

We celebrate with food.

GA1432

Different people have different celebrations.

19

Clothes

Clothes include all the different garments, accessories, and ornaments worn by people in the various parts of the world. They have become one of people's most important needs. Today more people wear clothing for decoration than for protection.

No one knows for sure when people first wore clothing, but it was probably more than 100,000 years ago. Early people probably wore clothing to protect themselves, to improve their appearance, and to tell people about themselves. Think about the hunter wearing a bearskin. It would tell others that he was a strong, skilled hunter and quite brave and strong.

By the end of the Stone Age (25,000 years ago), the needle had been invented and people could then sew skins together. Still all clothing was made by hand until quite recently. There were certainly no clothing factories. During the 1700's and 1800's the invention of the sewing machine took sewing out of the home and into the factories.

Children in most places in the world wear clothing. The type of clothing will vary depending on the need for protection, the access to different materials, knowledge of different methods for making clothes or different habits. Take a good look at the clothing in the various books you read to children. Let them talk about the similarities and differences. Typically the clothing varies due to the purpose of the clothing, the materials available, the ways of making clothes and the differences in customs. Gather traditional pieces of clothing from people in your community for the children to try on and examine. Pictures of traditional costumes are available in *The World Book Encyclopedia*, (1990), (Vol. 4, pp. 692-695).

Activities in this unit include sorting, matching, classifying, seriating, as well as games, races, art, songs, poems and general fun for all.

GA1432

All About My Clothes

Use the ditto sheet at the end of this unit to have the children draw pictures of themselves or pair up with partners who will draw pictures of them in the clothes that they have on today. On the back of the picture make two columns. Label one *protection*. Label the other *decoration*. List each piece of clothing in one column or the other.

Sorting Clothes

Bring in a large box or two of various types of clothing, both adult clothing and children's clothing, with as many cultures represented as you can. Have the children sort the clothing. Groups might include ages, need, cultural groups, protection/decoration.

What's in the Bag: A Relay

Fill two laundry bags with large-sized clothes and shoes. Place them at one end of the room. At the other end, put the children in two lines. The first child in the line runs to the bag, takes out one piece of clothing, puts it on and runs back to the group. The second runs to the bag and follows the same procedure. Continue until all have had a chance to get a piece of clothing.

Pair Up to Zip

When children are getting ready to go out to play, have them get their jackets, place them in a pile in the center of their circle and sit down. Assign children partners (at least each pair should have one who can zip). When you say "Pair Up to Zip," children are to get their jackets, put them on and help each other zip before they get in line in pairs to go outside. (If some don't zip, pair up to button.)

21

Tryin' on Clothes

Read Shel Silverstein's poem "Tryin' on Clothes" in *A Light in the Attic* (Harper & Row Publishers). Place a large box of clothes in an area of the room where children may dress up. Remember that it is safer to have larger-sized children's clothing in this area than adult clothing. Remember to provide as many pieces of clothing from occupations and different cultures as you can.

Provide a mirror, crayons and paper. Ask children to draw pictures of themselves or of each other in the clothes. (Photos are fun, too, if you keep a camera handy.) When all have accomplished this, give each child one picture that is not his own. His task is to find the clothing that the child had on from the picture that he has.

Children's Books

Ackerman, K. (1988). *Song and Dance Man*. New York: Alfred A. Knopf

Black, A.D. (1973). *A Woman of the Wood: A Tale from Old Russia*. New York: Holt, Rinehart and Winston.

Kruss, J. (1970). *The Tailor and the Giant*. New York: Platt & Munk Publishers.

Jacobsen, K. (1982). *Mexico (A New True Book)*. Chicago: Children's Press.

Margolies, B.A. (1990). *Rehema's Journey: A Visit in Tanzania*. New York: Scholastic, Inc.

Martin, P.M. (1968). *Kumi and the Pearl*.

Musgrove, M. (1976). *Ashanti to Zulu: African Traditions*. New York: Dial Books.

Silverstein, S. (1981). *A Light in the Attic*. New York: Harper & Row Publishers.

Steptoe, J. (1987). *Mufaro's Beautiful Daughters*. New York: Lothrop, Lee & Shepard Books.

How Many? What Kind?

Tell about all the different kinds of clothes you have on.

How many shoes do you have on? _____

What kind of shoes do you have on? _____
How many pieces of clothing do you have on?
_____

How many pieces of clothing do you have on that no one can see? _____

How long is your shoelace? _____
How many different colors do you have on?
_____

Do you have on any dots? _____
What color are your dots? _____

Do you have on any stripes? _____
What color are your stripes?

_____

_____

_____

_____

What clothing do you have on for decoration?

_____

_____

_____

_____

What is the favorite thing you have on?

_____

Me

Draw a picture of yourself here.

Name_____

Look at the clothes that you have on today. Draw a picture of yourself with just the clothes that you have on. Draw only the clothing that you can see. Label each piece of clothing in your picture.

If you have time, fold the paper in half. On the back label one half "Protection"; label the other half "Decoration." List your clothes in the right places.

24

GA1432

Clothes Take-Home Book

Read the story. Color the pictures. Cut out the boxes. Put the pictures in order.
Staple them together. Make a cover. Read the story to a friend. Take it home.
Read it to someone at home.

A soccer player wears
these clothes.

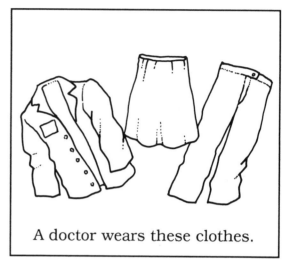

A doctor wears these clothes.

A teacher wears these clothes.

A dancer wears these clothes.

A painter wears these clothes.

I wear these clothes.

GA1432

These are the clothes I've learned about.

26

Corn

Today's corn puzzles botanists. They are unable to find its ancestor. It has to be cultivated, and it has been impossible to find its wild relatives. The top of the cornstalk has a tassel which grows pollen. Ears have filaments called silks which receive pollen. Because ears are wrapped in leaves and silks protrude only from the top, corn needs lots of neighbors to receive pollen—thus the need for cultivation. Today's corn was already being cultivated when the first explorers arrived. Its wild ancestor probably came from the Western Hemisphere.

When the white explorers first came to the Americas, they found corn with different colored kernels. The Native Americans liked to grow particular colors for particular purposes. As time went along the pioneers came to prefer the yellow corn for field corn.

Corn still comes in white, yellow, red, and blue. There are over 1000 varieties. The chief types are pod, soft, sweet, pop, fling and dent. The corn of the United States, Canada, and Australia is Indian corn or "maize." Most corn in the U.S. is grown in the corn belt—Iowa, Illinois, Indiana, Minnesota, Nebraska, and Ohio. It is grown in many other countries, but it is a major product in Central and South America, around the Mediterranean, in India and South Africa. Some is produced in China, Russia, Yugoslavia, Romania, Mexico, Italy, Hungary, Indonesia and France.

All I Know About Corn

Three of the books in the book list at the end of this article talk about corn and its uses (*The Popcorn Book*, *Corn Is Maize*, and *Three Stalks of Corn*). After reading one or all of these books, give each child a paper to fold into four boxes and draw four different ways that he eats corn. When he has the boxes done, label each, cut them out, and put his name on the back of each one.

Sort the pictures into like piles and place them in lines on the floor to make a graph. See which ways are most often used.

Each child can then take his own pieces of paper back and make them into a corn book.

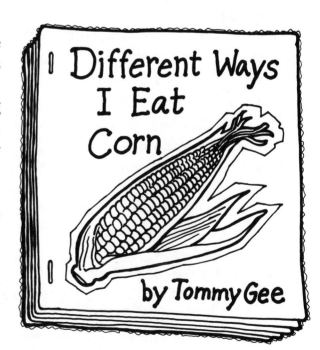

GA1432

How Many Types

Bring corn into the classroom in as many forms as you can find. Try corn on the cob, decorative corn, canned yellow corn, cream style corn, corn soup, popped corn, unpopped yellow popcorn, un-popped white popcorn, cheese corn, caramel corn, tortillas, cornmeal, corn chips, blue corn chips, corn muffins, frozen corn as starters.

Label each of the products you bring into the classroom. Give the children paper and pencils and let them make lists of ways they have eaten corn. Older children might make a three-column list–Ways I Like to Eat Corn, Ways I Don't Like to Eat Corn, Ways to Eat Corn I Haven't Tried.

Conclude this with a tasting party. Eat it all up.

Tortillas

Let the children make tortillas. Most Hispanic stores now have tortilla mix already packaged and all you have to do is add water, smash thin, and grill. Eat plain or with beans, cheese, lettuce, and tomatoes.

Be sure to set up some playdough in the housekeeping center to reinforce what you are doing.

If you have a Hispanic resource person, ask him to come into the class and work with your children.

How Much Will It Make?

Place four to five different-sized bowls on a table with $1/2$ cup (120 ml) of unpopped corn. Have each child place a piece of paper with his name on it next to the bowl he thinks will be just right for the popped corn. Pop the $1/2$ cup (120 ml) of corn. Pour it into bowls, starting with the largest and moving to the smallest. See who was right. Eat up.

GA1432

Where Will It Land?

Sew together two large sheets and place them in the center of your circle area. Place a cutting board in the center with a popcorn popper or electric skillet on it.

Gather all the children around you in a circle asking them to make a very large circle around the outside of the sheet.

Place a few pieces of popcorn–at least one per child–in the popper and leave the lid off. Allow the children to watch what you are doing and ask them what they think will happen. Have them observe closely to see where the kernels land.

After this first exercise, give each child a piece of paper. Have him put his name on it and place it where he thinks the most pieces will land.

Place the maximum amount of popcorn in the popper. Sit back. Watch; observe; comment. When the popping is all done, have each child carry his sheet of paper to the table and count the kernels, glue them to the paper and put the number in the corner. Leave them on the tables to dry. Compare amounts with each other. Take them home to help tell parents about what happened in school today.

Return to the sheet. Start at the outside edge and eat your way to the middle.

Tossing Corn

Place a line about 3 feet (.91 m) from two large empty bowls. Near the line, place a bowl of unpopped corn (mark a 1 on the edge of it) and a bowl of popped corn (mark a 5 on it). Have the children throw the corn into the empty bowls and tally the number of points that they get–1 for each unpopped kernel and 5 for each popped kernel. Listen to the comments and try to help them find answers to their questions.

Children's Books

Aliki. (1976). *Corn Is Maize: The Gift of the Indians*. New York: Thomas Y. Crowell Company.

Clark, A.N. (1941, 1969). *In My Mother's House*. New York: The Viking Press.

De Paola, T. (1978). *The Popcorn Book*. New York: Scholastic, Inc.

Lattimore, D.N. (1991). *The Flame of Peace: A Tale of the Aztecs*. Harper Trophy.

Politi, L. (1976). *Three Stalks of Corn*. New York: Charles Scribner's Sons.

Rylant, C. (1982). *When I Was Young in the Mountains*. New York: E.P. Dutton & Co., Inc.

Cornhusk Dolls

Materials

    $1\frac{1}{2}$" (1.25 cm) Styrofoam ball per student
    several packages of cornhusks
    parcel string

To Begin

    Soak the cornhusks in water until they are soft and pliable.
    Ask for parents to volunteer with the tying, especially with younger children.

What to Do

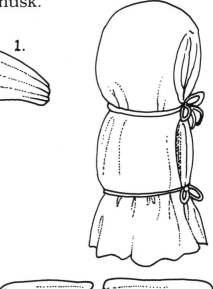

1. Wrap one Styrofoam ball with one cornhusk.

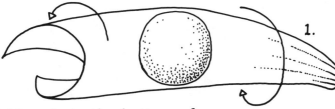

2. Fold ends to the bottom of the ball. Gather together. Tie with string to form the head, neck, and base of the torso.

3. Fold another cornhusk into thirds from the ends of the husk. Gather and tie with string about $\frac{1}{2}$" (1.25 cm) from each end. This will form the arms of the doll.

4. Slip the arms between the loose ends of the head/ neck section, pushing them tightly against the neck. Secure the arms by tightly tying the ends beneath them with string.

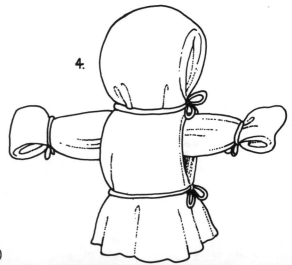

GA1432

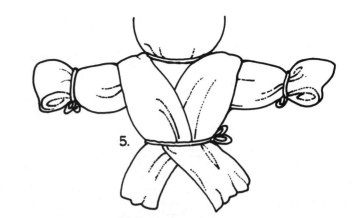

5. Make a bodice by laying a cornhusk over each shoulder and crisscrossing the ends. Secure at the waist with string.

6. Place several layers of cornhusks over the torso and the head of the doll with the narrow ends covering the shoulders and head of the doll as shown below. Place the layers on both the front and the back of the doll. Secure at the waist tightly with string.

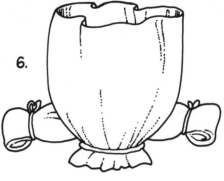

7. Gently pull the layers of cornhusks down to form the doll's skirt.

8. Add Spanish moss for hair and draw a face with a fine tip permanent marker if desired.

Other Suggestions
* Make the dolls out of creative twist paper ribbon.
* Let older children make clothes for their dolls using scraps of material, felt, ribbon, and yarn.
* Boy dolls can be made by slitting the skirt down the middle and tying each side with string 1/2" (1.25 cm) from the ends.

Thanks to Gaye Ruschen's grandmother.

GA1432

Corn Take-Home Book

Read the story. Color the pictures. Cut out the boxes. Put the pictures in order. Staple them together. Make a cover. Read the story to a friend. Take it home. Read it to someone at home.

This is corn in a dish.

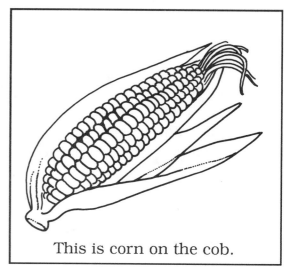

This is corn on the cob.

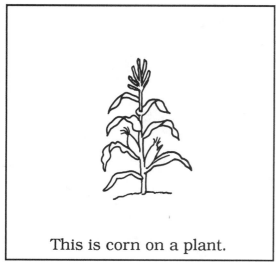

This is corn on a plant.

This is cornmeal.

This is corn oil.

This is my favorite kind of corn.

GA1432

Corn is used in many ways by many people.

33

Dads

The word *dad* is a nickname for one's father. According to *Webster's Ninth New Collegiate Dictionary* it probably originated from baby talk. The term *father* is used in a number of different ways. All of these ways, however, use the term to refer to an adult male who is in an authoritative or respected position. In this unit we will use it to refer to the older male figure in a household who is in a position of authority over members of the household. This older male is also the male that sired the child/children or is their father by adoption or by a marriage to the child's/children's mother.

In many early societies the father or dad was the most powerful figure in the family. This still exists in some cultures today. Men held the most power because they produced the family's wealth. However, some societies and cultures have adoped a system which gives men and women equal power in the family. Today, the women in families often contribute directly to the family's income and therefore share in how that family's wealth is used and are able to help in the decision making.

Dads and moms play a major role in a process called socialization by which children learn to become independent members of society. When the dad is present, he is the male role model for his children.

In this day and age, we must be aware of the family structure of each of our children. Some may have dads in the home. Others may have dads that they visit frequently. Some may have dads they have never known or seen. Some may have adult male role models who are uncles, brothers, grandfathers. Some may have no adult male role models close to home. Be careful how you address those issues.

My Dad and Me

Depending on the makeup of your class, ask each child either to bring in a photograph of his father or to draw or paint a picture of him. Post the pictures next to pictures of the children.

Just with Dad

Ask the children to talk about the things that they do with their dads. See if you can come up with a different thing for each child.

Give each child a piece of 9" x 12" (22.86 x 30.48 cm) paper to draw the picture on. Write about what they are doing at the bottom using one language pattern. "Dad and I _____." When finished, put into a class book and place in the reading corner.

GA1432

Dads at Home

At the end of this unit is a ditto sheet that asks children to work with the fathers to record some things that the fathers do at home. When this sheet is sent home, allow time for children to work with their fathers. If you have a high number of absent fathers, allow a two-week time period for completion.

When the children bring the sheets back, share with the group.

Have the children record the four things they know best on four slips of paper to make a class graph of things dads do at home.

A Promise Pocket

After the children show the results of what their dads do at home, have them think of ways that they could help their dads at home. Remember these might include helping, entertaining themselves, sweeping up, stacking, etc.

Make coupons for the children to take home to their dads to show them what they might promise to help their dads do.

Place the promise coupons in pockets for the children to take home.

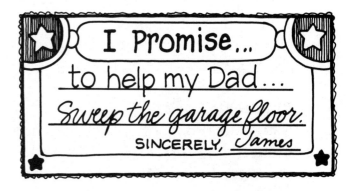

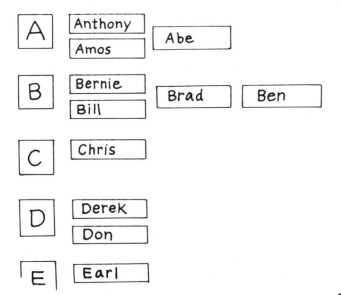

My Dad's Name

Have each child give you the name of his father and record it on a sheet of paper. Put a set of alphabet letters on the floor in a column. Each child then places his father's name by the right letter to see how many fathers' names start with each letter.

Dads at Work

Send home a paper sack with each child with a note attached to bring something to school in the sack that will tell about what his dad does at work. Place the child's name on the bottom of the sack where it cannot be seen when sitting on the floor.

When the children bring these to school, set them on the floor and mix them up. At circle time, have the children choose one sack to bring to the circle. Have the children open up one sack, tell what they can about what is there, and try to guess what the father's occupation is and whose father it might be. When they find out whose father it is, place the sack behind that child. Continue until all have had a turn. As a follow-up activity, have each child draw a picture of what he brought in his sack and write the occupation under the picture. Post on the bulletin board "Dads at Work."

Moms, Families and Grandparents

Refer to the sections on Moms (page 83), Families (page 46) and Grandparents (page 66) for other activities that include what the children do with their dads and moms; what dads and moms do at work, play, home and away; listing and alphabetizing names of parents; trips they take with their parents; ancestors; places of birth. In each case, use any of the activities suggested there and change the focus to dads.

Children's Books

Bang, M. (1983). *Ten, Nine, Eight.* New York: Greenwillow Books.

Caines, J. (1977). *Daddy.* New York: Harper & Row Publishers.

Feelings, M. (1974). *Jambo Means Hello: Swahili Alphabet Book.* New York: Dial.

Fufuka, K. (1975). *My Daddy Is a Cool Dude.* New York: The Dial Press.

Greenfield, E. (1976). *First Pink Light.* New York: Scholastic Book Services.

Isadora, R. (1991). *At the Crossroads.* New York: Greenwillow Books.

Margolies, B.A. (1990). *Rehema's Journey: A Visit in Tanzania.* New York: Scholastic, Inc.

Musgrove, M. (1976). *Ashanti to Zulu: African Traditions.* New York: Dial Books.

Surat, M.M. (1983). *Angel Child, Dragon Child.* New York: Scholastic, Inc.

Udry, J.M. (1966). *What Mary Jo Shared.* Chicago: Albert Whitman & Company.

Wyndham, R. (Ed.). (1968). *Chinese Mother Goose Rhymes.* Cleveland: The World Publishing Company.

GA1432

Dads at Home

Work with your parents to tell about what your dad does at home. You can use four photographs, draw four pictures, or write about four things.

GA1432

Dads Take-Home Book

Read the story. Draw the pictures. Cut out the boxes. Put the pictures in order. Staple them together. Make a cover. Read the story to a friend. Take it home. Read it to someone at home.

My dad	My dad in the morning
My dad at night	My dad at work
My dad is playing.	My dad and me

38

Different dads do different things.

Drums

The drum, the oldest musical instrument, is a member of the percussion family of instruments. It is played by striking it with the hand, sticks, or other blunt objects. The different types of drums are snare, bass, kettle, and steel. All of these are used to produce different sounds and for different kinds of musical performances.

Several other instruments are members of the drum family. The tambourine is a metal hoop with metal disks on the rim and a thin membrane stretched across one side. It can be played by shaking or striking it on the hand or leg, for example. It was made popular by Turkish soldiers from the 1400's to the early 1800's. Western musicians began using them in the 1700's.

The tom-tom is a cylinder with a thin sheet of plastic or calfskin called a head stretched across the top, bottom, or both. It measures from 6" to 18" (15.24 to 45.72 cm) inches in diameter and stands from 6" to 20" (15.24 to 50.8 cm) high. The tom-tom produces a dull hollow sound and may be tuned by adjusting the tightness of the heads. Tom-toms are played with felt mallets, drumsticks, or with the hands. The earliest tom-toms were animal skins stretched across a hollow log.

Bongo drums, called bongos, are rhythm instruments in Latin-American music that produce a high-pitched sound. Bongos are played in pairs. The two drums are attached at the center. One of the drums has a smaller diameter to produce a higher-pitched sound.

The conga drum is also a Latin-American rhythm instrument which was developed from an ancient African drum. It is a slightly rounded cylinder made of wood and fiberglass with animal skins covering the head. It is played by striking the head with fingers and the hand.

The drum has also been used to communicate messages over long distances. Thousands of years before the telegraph was invented people knew that sound traveled faster than the fastest runner or horse. Drums or hollow logs were used to send messages to other people who understood the code used by the sender. While fires and smoke signals were also used to send messages over long distances, the drum could communicate more complicated messages than those communicated by fire and smoke.

Horn blasts, gunshots, and ringing bells were later used by some people to send messages over long distances. Today, telephone bells, doorbells, sirens, and automobile horns are used to send messages to people.

What's a Drum?

A drum is a member of the percussion (to be hit) family of instruments played by striking with the hand, sticks or other objects.

Collect as many drums as you can. If you have an instrumental or vocal music teacher, ask him to come in to demonstrate the official use of the drums. Let the children try each of the drums out to listen to the different sounds they make.

When they are familiar with the sounds, ask them to identify them without seeing which one is being played. Children can work in pairs to do this.

What's the Sound of the Big Bass Drum?

Measure the sizes of the various drums to see what sounds the small ones make when compared to the large ones.

What Sound Does It Make?

Collect various hollow things for the children to listen to and identify. Try oatmeal cartons, Crisco cans, tins, margarine containers, coffee cans, Pringles cans, Planters cans. These containers may be tried right side up and bottom side up to determine if the sounds are the same or different.

After determining the quality of sound from the bottom or top, try comparing two different types. Give each child a different carton and pair him/her up with a friend. When they have compared and contrasted those sounds, switch partners.

Drums of Our Own

Let the children make drums of their own. Use circular pieces of vinyl, oilcloth, canvas, or chamois, to place over the end of cans which have had both ends cut out. Younger children will need help attaching these pieces of vinyl with rubber bands. Older children can punch holes in the vinyl and stitch the two pieces together, being careful not to pull tight enough to tear the material, but tight enough to give a sound to the drum head.

Compare the sounds made by each of their drums with others' and with the hollow objects mentioned above. Let them try to explain the difference in the sounds.

How Far Away?

A drum was used for communication over long distances. Take a drum outside. Let one child play it in a consistent manner while the others scatter until they cannot hear the drum. Measure the distance that the children can hear the drum.

GA1432

Trick the Dancers

Located in the book *Games from Many Lands* is a game similar to Freeze. Dancers dance while the drum drums. When the drum stops, the dancers freeze. Those who do not are out.

How Long Will It Take?

People used drums to communicate because they found out that sound travelled faster than the fastest runner. Place one child with a' drum to beat out a message. Give a second child a written message. Place the third child out in the field. See which message gets to the third child first.

Rhythms

Let the children play different rhythms on their drums individually and have the class respond to the rhythm. Fast might mean to run, slow might mean to crawl, etc.

Play the rhythm of a familiar song for the children with no melody and no words. See if they can tell you what song you are beating.

Types and Uses of Drums

Following is a list of multicultural books that contain information about and pictures of drums. Give one book to each small group of children. Have them find the pictures of the drums and talk about how the drum is being used. Have them illustrate the drum and write about its use. Share information from group to group.

Children's Books

Agard, J. (1989). *The Calypso Alphabet.* New York: Henry Holt and Company.

Benarde, A. (1970). *Games from Many Lands.* New York: The Lion Press.

Cohlene, T. (1990). *Dancing Drum: A Cherokee Legend.* Mahwah, NJ: Watermill Press.

Hoyt-Goldsmith, C. (1991). *Pueblo Storyteller.* New York: Holiday House.

Isadora, R. (1991). *At the Crossroads.* New York: Greenwillow Books.

Lessac, F. (1987). *My Little Island.* New York: Harper Trophy.

Waters, K., and Slovenz-Low, M. (1990). *Lion Dancer: Ernie Wan's Chinese New Year.* New York: Scholastic, Inc.

How Far?

Cut out the pictures and put them in order from near to far. If you can, make more boxes to put other forms of communication in the right places.

43

Drums Take-Home Book

Read the story. Color the pictures. Cut out the boxes. Put the pictures in order. Staple them together. Make a cover. Read the story to a friend. Take it home. Read it to someone at home.

These are snare drums.

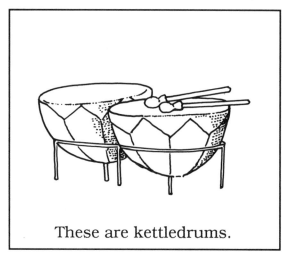

These are kettledrums.

These are bongo drums.

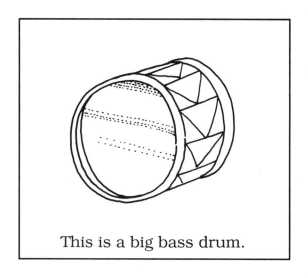

This is a big bass drum.

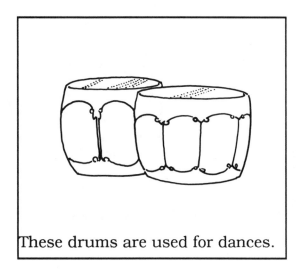

These drums are used for dances.

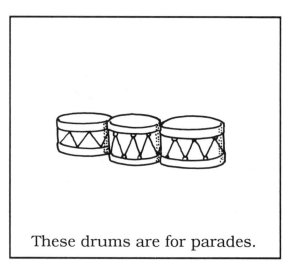

These drums are for parades.

GA1432

Different people use different drums in different ways.

45

GA1432

Families

The family is the oldest and most common human institution. Most people grow up in a family and, as adults, establish a family of their own. Generally a family is defined as a group of related persons who share a common home. It also is a term that refers to all of a person's ancestors and other relations. Most families are based on kinship, i.e. the members belong to the same family through birth, marriage, or adoption.

The term *nuclear family* refers to the parents and their children. The extended family household includes the married children, their spouses, and their offspring. Aunts, uncles, and cousins could also belong to the extended family household. The extended family (not living in the same household) would include all members who are related by birth, marriage, or adoption. Adopted children have the same legal rights that children by birth have in a family.

Clans are recognized in some cultures. A clan consists of all the people descended from a common ancestor through the mother's or father's side of the family. The functions of the family unit in society varies from culture to culture. In most societies it is the social unit that provides protection and training for the children, teaches the children the culture of the society, provides economic support, and is a means of preserving property by the children becoming heirs to parents' land and other wealth.

In industralized societies families generally meet the emotional and social needs of the family members. Each member is expected to provide the others with affection, emotional support, and a sense of belonging. Family members are adopting new roles. Over the last fifty years the number of employed married women in the United States has risen from 15 percent (1940) to 55 percent (1990). This has led to the ideal of the equalitarian family, i.e. each member is respected and neither parent tries to be the head of the family. Divorce has also increased dramatically in industralized countries, and this accounts for many single mothers working outside the home in order to support the family.

The home in industralized countries is the center of family activities. Caring for and teaching the children, playing games, watching television, reading, cooking, keeping house, entertaining friends all take place in the home. Children learn basic social skills, health and safety habits from their parents in the family home. Family meals are the major source of nutrition.

Tradition, laws, and social conditions help determine who lives in a home and the place each family member holds in all societies.

GA1432

A Family Portrait

Have each child bring in a picture of himself or save one from the school pictures. Glue the picture onto an oval piece of paper. Ask the child to draw the rest of the family in the picture, putting them in order (of height or age, whichever the child chooses).

Have the children tell and show you their place in their families. After they look at the whole family, cover the adults with a piece of paper and ask them what their place is among the children.

Make a frame for the picture or mount it on construction paper. Cover with glitter to "gold leaf."

What's My Job?

Talk about the jobs that children have in the classroom. Have them then tell you what kinds of jobs that they have to do at home. (A related ditto sheet for the whole family is at the end of this unit.)

Give each child a piece of paper and fold it into four squares. In each square have him draw one of the jobs that he does at home. Label each square. When the children have finished, let them share their jobs with the group.

After sharing, cut the paper into the four boxes. Have the child put his name on the back of each. Group the activities together and put them in rows to show how many do each job. Tape them to a piece of chart paper to make a graph.

What Does Your Family Do Together?

Send home the "What the _____ Family Does" ditto sheet at the end of this unit. Ask the parents to work with the children to determine what types of things the family does together. When the children bring these back to school, have them share their pictures with one another and then post them in the classroom. This family work sheet will give information about what the family does at work, play, home and away. You may gain insight into the celebrations and traditions of the families.

Mealtime

Provide a stack of different colors of construction paper and have each child choose a color to match the area of his house where he eats dinner—the table, the tablecloth, the carpet, the floor.

Have children show with rectangles (place mats for tables or TV trays) or circles (plates for holding on their laps) where the various family members sit when they eat. Label each piece with the family member's name. Other key pieces of furniture can be glued in place.

Older children can then write on the plates/place mats/TV trays, what each person does before and/or after the meal. This will give you and them information about other job responsibilities of the family members.

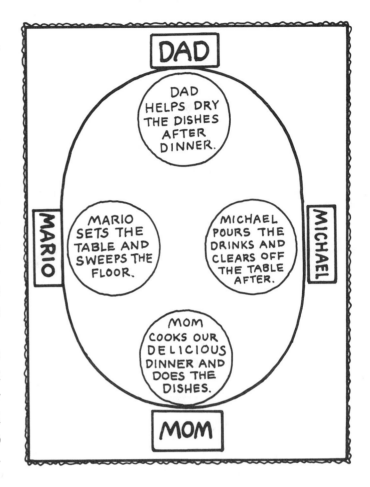

Just for Fun

Give each child a set of small pieces of paper. Discuss with them at circle time the types of activities that they do at home with their families that are just for fun, indoor and outdoor games, reading, relaxing, watching TV together, etc.

On the pieces of paper have the child draw a sequence of pictures showing the activity, how it starts, how it is played, and how it is finished.

When these are finished, pair up the children and let one child from each group place his pictures on the floor in sequence as he tells his story to another child. Switch roles. After the two children have shared their stories, switch pairs and let the children retell their stories to others.

To extend the activity:

Make a list of all the activities generated by the children.

Graph the activities to determine which activities are done by the most families and by the least families.

Group the children physically by the activities done.

Whose Shoe?

Make up a little sack of things for each child to take home. Include a crayon, a pair of scissors, several pieces of paper and the directions for the activity.

At home each child should trace around the feet of each member of his family. On each footprint have the parents write: Huong's Dad's Foot, naming each member of the family and relationship to the child.

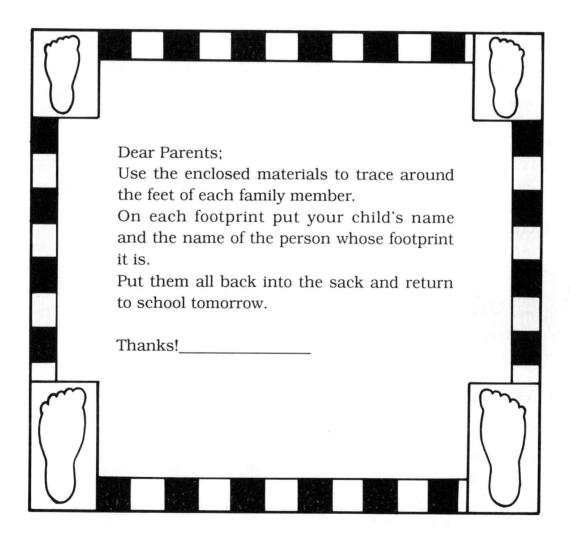

Dear Parents;
Use the enclosed materials to trace around the feet of each family member.
On each footprint put your child's name and the name of the person whose footprint it is.
Put them all back into the sack and return to school tomorrow.

Thanks!_____

GA1432

Moms and Dads

Refer to the sections on Moms (page 83) and Dads (page 34) for other activities that include what the children do with their dads and moms; what dads and moms do at work, play, home and away; listing and alphabetizing names of parents; trips they take with their parents; ancestors; places of birth.

What's in a Family?

List the letters of the word *family* down the left-hand side of a piece of chart paper. Have the children think of things that describe families or their families specifically that start with each of the letters. Write the words and draw simple illustrations so that the children can "read" the words.

To follow up, give each child a piece of paper folded into six lines. Have them write the letters of the word *family* down the far left-hand side of the paper, one letter per line. Next to the letter, have them write/draw pictures describing families and family activities. They can use the chart to get ideas, or they can generate their own.

Family Collage

Give each child a piece of paper. Write the word *family* around all edges. Provide magazines, scissors and glue to cut out pictures from the magazines of the things he does with his families to glue onto the piece of paper. It is critical that you have magazines that have pictures of all races of children and parents in them.

Weekdays and Weekends

Give each child a large piece of paper folded into three to four boxes horizontally and two boxes vertically. In the top set of boxes, have the child draw what his family does, from the beginning to the end of the day, on a weekday. If each family member is at a different task, divide one box into four to five boxes with crayons, placing each person in a different box. Use the bottom boxes for the weekend. Compare weekday to weekend.

Children's Books

De Garza, P. (1973). *Chicanos: The Story of Mexican Americans*. New York: Julian Messner.

St. John, J. (1987). *A Family in Peru*. Minneapolis, MN: Lerner Publications Co. (A series of at least twenty-four books about families in various countries and of various cultures including Aboriginal, Arab, Australia, Bolivia, Brazil, Chile, China, Egypt, Eskimo, France, India, Ireland, Italy, Jamaica, Japan, Liberia, Morocco, Nigeria, Pakistan, Peru, Singapore, Sri Lanka, West Germany, Zulu.)

What the _____ Family Does

At home		
Away		
At work		
At play		

Draw pictures or write about what your family does at home, away, at work or play.

51

GA1432

Families Take-Home Book

Read the story. Draw the pictures. Cut out the boxes. Put the pictures in order.
Staple them together. Make a cover. Read the story to a friend. Take it home.
Read it to someone at home.

My family

My family in the morning

My family at night

My family in the car

My family at the movie

My family visiting school

These are the different families I learned about.

53

Flowers

Flowers are used in most countries and are available in all sorts of climates and terrains. They grow almost anywhere, in deserts, jungles, yards, along roadsides and on snow-covered mountains. To try to name or sort these flowers would be time consuming. There are over 250,000 varieties of flowering plants.

Although we mostly use flowers for their beauty, different groups of people use flowers for different things. Some use them for decoration, celebrations, feasts and festivals, as gifts and in mourning. Flowers are admired for their beauty, but their true value is their reproductive value. The flower blossom makes seeds.

Flowers provide an experience in cultures and families as well as in science and literature. The activities provided cover children's awareness of flowers in their environment, their families' use of flowers, a few scientific experiments with flowers, and some literature-based, follow-up activities.

Watch the Flowers

When you study flowers, be sure that you stress to the children that there are many different kinds of flowers. In essence we are telling them that there are many different kinds of flowers, people, toys or work. We continually ask them to compare and contrast each of these things.

Ask the children to watch out for flowers in their surroundings and record the flowers and locations when they find them. Post these flowers and locations on a bulletin board entitled "Can You Find These Flowers?"

GA1432

Dried up Flowers

The purpose of a flower is to provide seeds to continue the line. These seeds can easily be seen when the flower is allowed to dry up and children can take them apart to see what the seeds look like.

Flowers will need to go without water for one to two weeks and still may not be dry enough. Marigolds and zinnias are two of the best to provide seeds that the children can examine. Be careful as the flowers are taken apart. Try to count how many seeds one flower produces.

Flowers at Home

Send home the work sheet at the end of this unit. Have the parents record when their family uses or gets flowers, one use on each flower.

When the children return the flowers, provide a class graph and let each student put a flower with his name on it in a square to show how his family uses flowers.

Categories for use might include birthdays, Valentine's Day, funerals, etc.

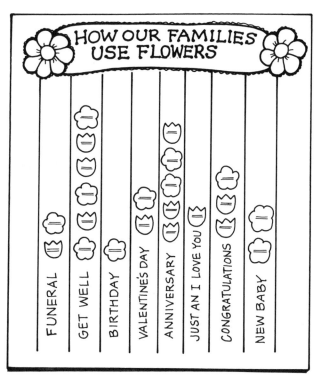

Do Flowers Drink?

Children love to watch the carnations change colors right before their eyes–or somewhat before their eyes.

Purchase a dozen white carnations for the children to experiment with. Place one in a jar with red food coloring. (The more you water it down, the less color and the slower it will go up the stem.) Place another in yellow, blue, and green. Place one in clear water in order to have a control.

To show the children how these are "pipes" that the water goes up is easiest through a piece of celery. Place the celery in food coloring and after the coloring has gone to the top, cut the celery in slices. They can see the "tubes" the water has passed through.

To show the children that there are many pipes/tubes in a stem, cut the carnation stem lengthwise and place one part of the stem in red food coloring and the other in blue food coloring. Watch what happens. Make flowers for your local athletic team by mixing colors and making duo or tri-colored flowers.

A Garden of Children

Kindergarten is actually translated as a "garden of children." Let each child make a large tissue paper flower of his favorite shape and colors. Cut artist tissue into 1" (2.54 cm) squares. Provide a variety of flower shapes for the children to trace around. Use watered-down glue to glue the tissue paper on and let the small pieces bleed.

When these are dry, glue a picture of the child in the center of the flower. Place the flowers on a bulletin board, making the stems out of green pipe cleaners and the leaves out of green feathers.

Using Children's Books

Several of the books listed below show how various cultures use flowers. In *Josephine's 'magination*, Josephine makes a doll from a flower and a stick. *The Gift of Hawaii* shows a lei made of flowers. *The Empty Pot* is about growing flowers from seed. In *The Paper-Flower Tree* a child tries to water a paper flower only to find it doesn't grow. Each one of these stories calls for a follow-up activity trying to do the same type of thing in the classroom.

Children's Books

Ayer, J. (1962). *The Paper-Flower Tree*. New York: Harcourt, Brace & World, Inc.

Bannon, L. (1961). *The Gift of Hawaii*. Chicago: Albert Whitman & Company.

Demi. (1990). *The Empty Pot*. New York: Henry Holt and Company.

Dempsey, M.W., and Sheehan, A. (1970). *How Flowers Live*. New York: Grolier Enterprises, Inc., The Danbury Press.

De Paola, T. (1983). *The Legend of the Bluebonnet*. New York: G.P. Putnam's Sons.

De Paola, T. (1988). *The Legend of the Indian Paintbrush*. New York: G.P. Putnam's Sons.

Dorbin, A. (1973). *Josephine's 'magination: A Tale of Haiti*. New York: Scholastic, Inc.

Feeney, S. (1985). *Hawaii Is a Rainbow*. Honolulu: University of Hawaii Press.

Keats, E.J. (1966). *Jennie's Hat*. New York: Harper & Row Publishers.

When We Use Flowers

On each of the flowers write one time that your family gets, gives, or uses flowers.

GA1432

Flowers Take-Home Book

Read the story. Color the pictures. Cut out the boxes. Put the pictures in order. Staple them together. Make a cover. Read the story to a friend. Take it home. Read it to someone at home.

These flowers are on the table.

These flowers are for the hair.

I made a doll out of this flower.

I made a necklace out of these flowers.

I made a crown out of these flowers.

These are my favorite flowers.

GA1432

Different people use flowers in different ways.

Foods

Studying different cultural groups provides an excellent opportunity for studying foods. Families may have some family foods–those that have traditionally been served in their families for generations. Different types of foods may be purchased in the stores. These foods, in addition to the regular foods seen and eaten by young children, can provide great learning experiences.

Field Trip

Begin or end this unit with a trip to the grocery store or market in your area. Plan ahead of time with the children behaviors that will be expected of them, what will be purchased, and who will be responsible for what. Make sure there are enough adults to make groups of four children per adult. Take an extra adult along for emergencies.

Plan to purchase foods to sort, for recipes, for examination, for seed hunts, and of various colors. Beside each of the following activities needing foods from the grocery, there will be a grocery list. Check it as you get ready for the trip.

On My Plate

In order to find out about what the children eat at home, have them take home the plate ditto at the end of this unit; and after they eat dinner at home, draw pictures of the foods that they ate. Parents may help them make a list of the foods on the back of the sheet.

When the children bring the sheet back to school, have them tell about what they had for dinner. Graph the foods to see how many children ate the same/different foods.

Have each child cut out a plate and mount it on a rectangular piece of paper to use as a place mat. He can use tin foil to cut out a knife, fork and spoon and glue on a paper cup at the right spot. Post on the bulletin board.

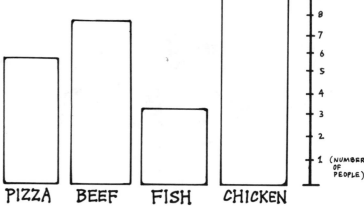

PIZZA   BEEF   FISH   CHICKEN

GA1432

Pass the Orange

In the book *Games from Many Lands*, the game of Pass the Orange (Ireland) is described. Children pass the orange from one person to another from neck to neck, trying not to drop it.

Food Rhymes

The book *Chinese Mother Goose Rhymes* contains rhymes about foods.

Everyone Eats Rice

Read the story *Everyone Cooks Rice* to the children. Plan to have a rice feast in the classroom with various rice dishes served, both cold and hot. The book itself has many different recipes in it. For most of them you could combine the other ingredients and serve over rice. Children could then choose any number of toppings to eat with the rice.

Food Festival

Experience the cultures of the children in your classroom or in your age group. Ask several of the parents to cook dishes from their own cultures, foods that have been eaten in their families for generations. At lunch one day, have the parents come into a large commons area and set up serving tables with decorations from the country or family each food comes from. Serve the foods to the children in small portions, encouraging them to taste the foods.

At each table have the parents provide a copy of the recipe. If the child likes the food, he can take home a copy of the recipe after he draws a picture of what it looks like. Then make all the recipes into a Food Festival Recipe Book.

Gift Books of Family Recipes

Send home a call for family recipes of the foods you are discussing. Let each child illustrate his family recipe. Compile into books for the children to give their parents as gifts.

As a cultural event, request that each family send one food a day for as many days as you have children and send along the recipes. Have the children taste the foods, illustrate the recipes, and send them home in gift books.

In this book there are specific units on harvest, corn, potatoes, and peanuts. These units also offer suggestions about foods and studying about them.

Roll It and Pat It and Mark It with a B

Give children playdough, plastic knives, small rolling pins, and pencils. Children roll out the playdough, cut out shapes of food with the plastic knives, and mark the food with beginning letters.

Place paper plates with alphabet letters on them in a central location. As children finish their foods, they take the foods and place them on the correct letters.

Variations: Cut pictures of foods out of newspaper ads or magazines and glue to the paper plate showing the beginning letter of the food.

Children's Books

Agard, J. (1989). *The Calypso Alphabet*. New York: Henry Holt and Company.

Appiah, S. (1988). *Amoko and Efua Bear*. New York: Macmillan Publishing Company.

Balet, J. (1969). *The Fence*. New York: Seymour Lawrence Delacorte Press.

Bannon, L. (1961). *The Gift of Hawaii*. Chicago: Albert Whitman & Company.

Benarde, A. (1970). *Games from Many Lands*. New York: The Lion Press.

Clark, A.N. (1941, 1969). *In My Mother's House*. New York: The Viking Press.

Dooley, N. (1991). *Everybody Cooks Rice*. Minneapolis, MN: Carolrhoda Books, Inc.

Duarte, M. (1968). *The Legend of the Palm Tree*. New York: Grosset & Dunlap Publishers.

Hoyt-Goldsmith, D. (1991). *Pueblo Storyteller*. New York: Holiday House.

Grifalconi, A. (1986). *The Village of Round and Square Houses*. Boston: Little, Brown and Company.

Jacobsen, K. (1982). *Mexico (A New True Book)*. Chicago: Children's Press.

Lessac, F. (1987). *My Little Island*. New York: Harper Trophy.

Margolies, B.A. (1990). *Rehema's Journey: A Visit in Tanzania*. New York: Scholastic, Inc.

Martel, C. (1976). *Yagua Days*. New York: The Dial Press.

Musgrove, M. (1976). *Ashanti to Zulu: African Traditions*. New York: Dial Books.

Nabwire, C., and Montgomery, B.V. (1988). *Cooking the African Way*. Minneapolis: Lerner Publications Company. (Twenty-one other books in the series.)

Stanek, M. (1989). *I Speak English for My Mom*. Niles, IL: Albert Whitman and Company.

Wyndham, R. (Ed.). (1968). *Chinese Mother Goose Rhymes*. Cleveland: The World Publishing Company.

Yashima, M., and Yashima, T. (1954). *Plenty to Watch*. New York: The Viking Press.

On My Plate

Dear Parents:
After dinner this evening, work with your child to draw pictures of the foods that he had for dinner on this plate. On the back make a list of the foods.

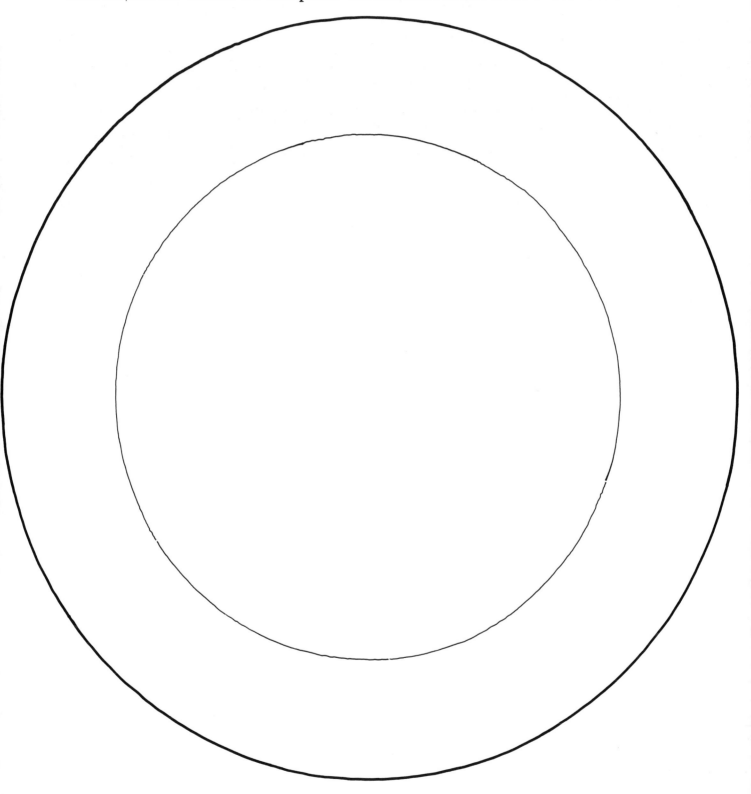

Foods Take-Home Book

Read the story. Color the pictures. Cut out the boxes. Put the pictures in order. Staple them together. Make a cover. Read the story to a friend. Take it home. Read it to someone at home.

These foods are red.

These foods are green.

These foods are yellow.

These foods are orange.

These are celebration foods.

These are my favorite foods.

GA1432

Foods can be fixed in many different ways.

Grandparents

Grandparents play different roles in different cultures. In the past with extended families, grandparents often lived with and ruled the families, with the elders being leaders. All younger people looked to their elders for guidance.

With increased mobility and communication systems, many families in this country are not as close as they once were. Some children may not even see their grandparents more than once every year. Others visit with them daily while the grandparents partake in the care of the children as support for families.

The relationship each of your children has with his grandparents will vary. You will find out what the relationships are as you continue through the unit.

Where in the World?

Post a world map, a U.S. map and a city map in the room. Send home a note to parents requesting information about the children's grandparents (see note at the end of the unit). Plot out the places where all the grandparents live by giving map pins and name tags to the students and having each place his name by where his grandparents live.

Review the information in several ways. Look at the number in the city, the state, the country, other countries. Graph the numbers for each. Graph occupations and recreational activities.

A Visit with Grandparents

During circle time have the children talk about how/when/why they visit grandparents. These discussions may include trips by car, on foot, by bus, by plane, by boat. They may be in summer, on holidays, or daily. They may be for child care, to visit, to celebrate.

Choose a mode of transportation specific to the way the child gets to his grandparents' home. Make this mode of transportation out of construction paper and write/draw about a visit with grandparents on the back.

GOING TO GRANDMA'S HOUSE

by Johny Wong

What Do Grandparents Do All Day?

Provide each child with a clock face divided into three parts, 10-2-6. Have children draw pictures or write about what their grandparents do in each part of the day. They can write their grandparents (see ditto at end) or interview them. Have children write back to their grandparents to tell them what they themselves do all day.

A Quilt Story

Read the story *The Patchwork Quilt* by Flournoy. Each square in the story quilt had its own story, a part of a special piece of clothing of someone in the family. Children can make quilt stories themselves. Give them several pieces of squares of paper to work with over a week or two. In each square each is to draw something special about himself, his parents or grandparents. After all squares are finished, have the child glue them onto a piece of construction paper or tagboard to take home or mail to grandparents, unattached, and suggest that they make a family quilt out of them by glueing them together.

Children's Books

Adoff, A. (1991). *Hard to Be Six*. New York: Lothrop, Lee & Shepard Books.

Belpre, P. (1969). *Santiago*. New York: Frederick Warne and Company, Inc.

Bonnici, P. (1985). *The Festival*. Minneapolis: Carolrhoda Books, Inc.

Flournoy, V. (1985). *The Patchwork Quilt*. New York: Dial Books for Young Readers.

Greenfield, E. (1980). *Grandmama's Joy*. New York: Collins.

Greenfield, E. (1988). *Grandpa's Face*. New York: Sandcastle Books (Putnam & Grosset Book Group).

Hoyt-Goldsmith, D. (1991). *Pueblo Storyteller*. New York: Holiday House.

Hoguet, S. (1983). *I Unpacked My Grandmother's Trunk*. New York: Dutton.

Hughes, M. (1967). *Why Carlo Wore a Bonnet*. New York: Lothrop, Lee & Shepard Books.

Johnson, A. (1990). *When I Am Old with You*. New York: Orchard Books.

Luenn, N. (1990). *Nessa's Fish*. New York: Atheneum.

Margolies, B.A. (1990). *Rehema's Journey: A Visit in Tanzania*. New York: Scholastic.

Miles, M. (1971). *Annie and the Old One*. Boston: Little, Brown and Company.

Nikola-Lisa, W. (1991). *Night Is Coming*. New York: Dutton Children's Books.

Rylant, C. (1982). *When I Was Young in the Mountains*. New York: E.P. Dutton & Co., Inc.

Tejima. (1990). *Ho-Limlim: A Rabbit Tale from Japan*. New York: Philomel Books.

Young, E. (1989). *Lon Po Po: A Red-Riding Hood Story from China*. New York: Scholastic, Inc.

Dear Parents:

During the next few days we will be studying grandparents. We would like some information from you. We will be writing to our grandparents and sending them some things we do. We will locate on maps where they live and talk about things they enjoy doing. In the end we will make a book about them and mail it directly to them. Thanks for your help.

Names of Grandparents _____   _____

Address _____   _____

City, State, ZIP _____   _____

Occupation _____   _____

Things they like to do _____   _____

Names of Grandparents _____   _____

Address _____   _____

City, State, ZIP _____   _____

Occupation _____   _____

Things they like to do _____   _____

Names of Grandparents _____   _____

Address _____   _____

City, State, ZIP _____   _____

Occupation _____   _____

Things they like to do _____   _____

Names of Grandparents _____   _____

Address _____   _____

City, State, ZIP _____   _____

Occupation _____   _____

Things they like to do _____   _____

Names of Grandparents _____   _____

Address _____   _____

City, State, ZIP _____   _____

Occupation _____   _____

Things they like to do _____   _____

GA1432

What Do I Do All Day?

Dear Grandparent:

We are studying grandparents. We were wondering what you do all day. Would you please write or draw some things that you do during these times of the day and mail it back to me? Thank you.

GA1432

Grandparents Take-Home Book

Read the story. Draw the pictures. Cut out the boxes. Put the pictures in order. Staple them together. Make a cover. Read the story to a friend. Take it home. Read it to someone at home.

Some of my grandparents	Some more of my grandparents
One grandparent cooking	One grandparent reading
My grandparents and me	Fun with my grandparents

Look at all the grandparents.

Homes

Shelter can be defined as "a structure or natural feature that provides protection against weather, danger, or insect pests." The first shelters made by humans were built of animal hides, stones, straw, vines, or wood.

People build many different types of shelters throughout the world. The different kinds they build generally depend on the climate of that region. Houses in hot areas have many screened openings (windows and doors) that let in breezes but keep out insect pests. Houses in cool areas are designed to keep out the cold and retain heat. Thick walls and storm windows reduce heat loss. Houses in snowy areas have sloping (steep) roofs so that snow will slide off easily. The roofs of these houses must be strong enough to hold the weight of heavy snow.

The kinds of building materials that are easily available often influence the kinds of houses constructed in a particular region. Regions with large forests will use wood to build houses because lumber is easy to build with. However, moisture can cause wood to rot within a few years. Therefore, in wet tropical areas such as Africa and many Pacific islands, people weave the stems of tall grasses into houses. People use clay and mud to build houses in areas with little rainfall. Adobe houses can be found in areas such as Mexico and southwestern United States. Clay shelters are often built in some areas of India. Builders almost everywhere can use concrete or bricks to build shelters. Industrialized countries build high-rise structures of steel and concrete. Almost every country in the world today has some steel and concrete structures. Prefabricated buildings use large amounts of plastic and other lightweight materials because the pieces are built at factories and then shipped to locations to be assembled.

Tradition sometimes influences the types of houses built. Latin American houses are often built out of adobe with tiled roofs showing the Portuguese and Spanish influence.

Special environmental hazards can also influence the kinds of shelters. Houses in Japan are often constructed of lightweight materials because of the prevalence of earthquakes. If an earthquake occurs and houses fall down, those living in them are less likely to be killed or seriously injured by heavy building materials. Houses erected on stilts are common in Indonesia, the Philippines, and other areas with swampland.

My Home

Ask children to bring in photos of their homes or suggest that you are able to take pictures of their homes. Bring them to school.

Have each child draw a picture of his home from the photograph.

Sort the homes into various types, letting the children name the groups–one-story, two-story, long, short, apartment, condominium etc.

What's in My City?

Most real estate agencies have pictures of homes that they publish weekly or monthly and place in grocery stores. Get four of these for your classroom. Cut out the pictures and mount them onto cards, making sure that there are two of each picture. Have the children find the matches, place into groups, and examine the various types of housing in your community.

If you have friends in different parts of the country, write and ask that they send you four magazines from their cities. Mount the pictures of houses on different colors of paper. Match them, group them, and then compare this city with yours.

Where's My Home?

Give each child a paper sack. Cut the paper sack off to be the right size proportionately to the child's house. Make it tall if he lives in an apartment or two-story house and shorter for a one-story house.

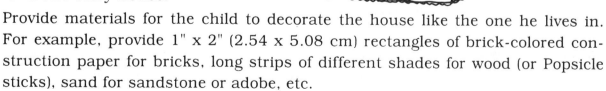

Provide materials for the child to decorate the house like the one he lives in. For example, provide 1" x 2" (2.54 x 5.08 cm) rectangles of brick-colored construction paper for bricks, long strips of different shades for wood (or Popsicle sticks), sand for sandstone or adobe, etc.

After the children have made their houses, have them stuff them with newspaper to allow them to stand up. Provide each child a piece of paper to fold in half for the roof. On each roof, write the child's address.

Locate each child's home on a city map or make a map of your neighborhood area and locate it on that map with a map pin and a name tag.

73

All Types of Houses

Different regions use different types of materials to build houses depending on the climate and availability of materials. In many of the books listed at the end of this unit, houses are shown.

At various places or tables put sets of building materials.

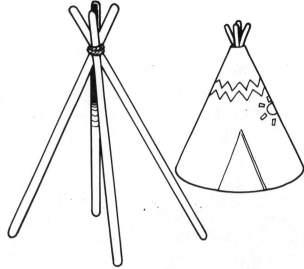

1. stones, dirt, water (brick or stone)
2. sticks, material, scissors, markers (teepees)
3. Lincoln Logs (the old days)
4. Popsicle sticks, wood glue (wooden houses)
5. ice cubes and salt (snowy areas)
6. sticks, grasses, glue (tropical areas)
7. Popsicle sticks, glue, and paper (Japan)

Place groups of children at each table and have them solve the problem of making one house from the materials that they have available. Talk with them about what types of weather these houses might survive in.

Children's Books

Brown, T. (1991). *Lee Ann: The Story of a Vietnamese-American*. New York: G.P. Putnam's Sons.

Cannon, C. (1971). *What I Like to Do*. New York: Coward, McCann & Geoghegan, Inc.

Clark, A.N. (1941, 1969). *In My Mother's House*. New York: The Viking Press.

Cohlene, T. (1990). *Dancing Drum: A Cherokee Legend*. Mahwah, NJ: Watermill Press.

Grifalconi, A. (1986). *The Village of Round and Square Houses*. Boston: Little Brown and Company.

Lessac, F. (1987). *My Little Island*. New York: Harper Trophy.

Levinson, R. (1988). *Our Home Is the Sea*. New York: E.P. Dutton & Co., Inc.

Margolies, B.A. (1990). *Rehema's Journey: A Visit in Tanzania*. New York: Scholastic, Inc.

Rylant, C. (1982). *When I Was Young in the Mountains*. New York: E.P. Dutton & Co., Inc.

Waters, K., and Slovenz-Low, M. (1990). *Lion Dancer*. New York: Scholastic, Inc.

Find Your Way Home

Draw your picture in the box in the upper left-hand corner. Then draw a picture of your home in the box in the lower right-hand corner. Begin at START and work your way through the maze to your home. In the spaces in the maze, draw things you would see on your way.

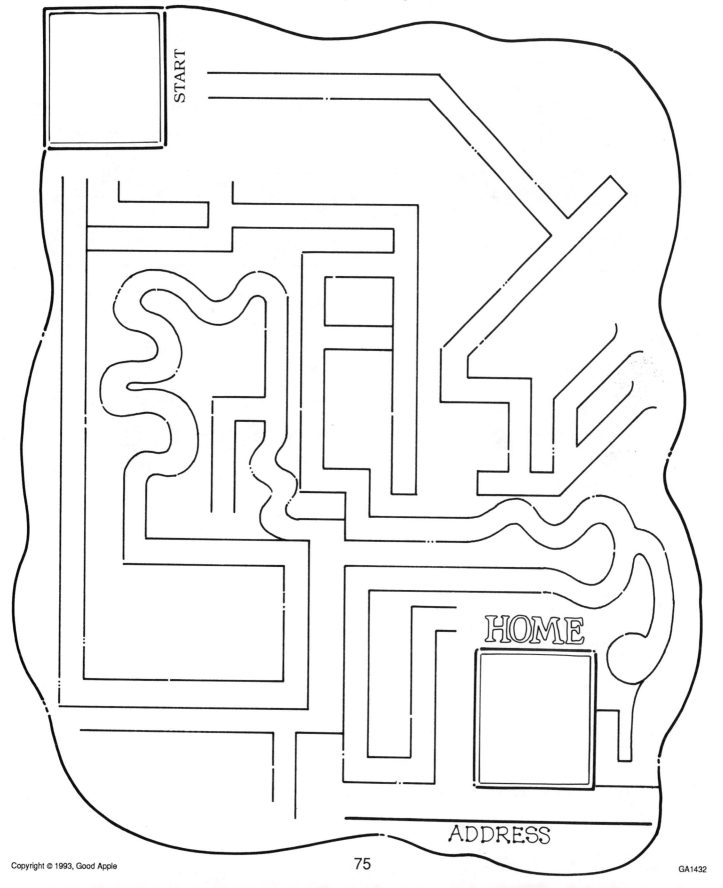

START

HOME

ADDRESS

75

Homes Take-Home Book

Read the story. Color the pictures. Cut out the boxes. Put the pictures in order. Staple them together. Make a cover. Read the story to a friend. Take it home. Read it to someone at home.

This home is made of grass.

This home is made of wood.

This home is made of adobe.

This home is made of logs.

This home is made of snow.

This is my home.

GA1432

People live in all types of homes.

77

Immigration/Moving

As stated in Dr. Huber's introduction, America is the home for as many as two thirds of the world's immigrants. This immigration was caused by moving, moving from one place to another. Today, people are still immigrating to America. In addition, many people in America are moving from one place to another. We are a mobile society, breaking from the traditions of the past where families stayed and grew in the same general area.

Many children from your classroom will move each year. They are anxious about the move. Other children can catch the anxiety and fear that their families, too, will be moving. Moving is traumatic for the family and therefore traumatic for the child, no matter how easy the move is made for them. The best thing is to examine the fact that all people have moved to get to where they are today. No one person in this country is still living where his ancestors did years and years ago. In our country the Native Americans would come the closest, but because of their forced moves, have left the land that they originally called home.

As with most of the other units in this book, activities begin close at home with things that are meaningful to the children and move into things a bit more abstract.

Let's Move

To start this unit, put aside a day where you will rearrange your room. Don't do it while the children are gone from the room; do it while they are there. It is a "Let's Move!" day.

Begin with a circle discussion of the need to rearrange the room and have the children offer suggestions. Discuss their pros and cons. Draw a picture of the way the room is at the present time. Use a map and moveable markers to rearrange the room visually first. Spend a lot of time moving their things and your things. Clean as you go. Relabel all things that need labelling. Check the room against the "map." Have the children draw "after" pictures of the room.

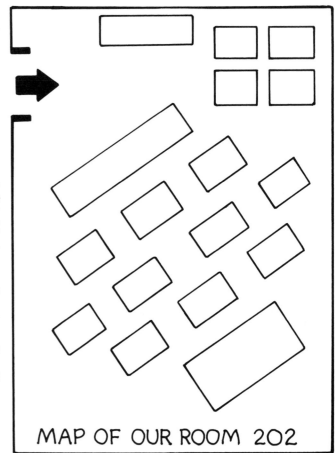

MAP OF OUR ROOM 202

GA1432

What to Pack

Give each child a piece of brown construction paper to use as a suitcase. He may decorate it anyway he wants. Tape it along the top edge to another piece of construction paper so that the top cover flips up. Inside is to be where he packs to move.

The instructions to the children are that it is moving day. They are moving to Florida. What will they take with them? Give them catalogs and magazines to cut out pictures as they pack for the move. Write *Florida* at the bottom of the page.

On another day, give them another piece of paper to tape to these first two. The children are now moving to Alaska. What will they take with them? Give them catalogs and magazines to cut out pictures as they pack for the move. Write *Alaska* at the bottom of the page.

Each time you talk about another country or place, you can add a page to your suitcase. Many of the children's books listed on the next page show different places children live, many with different climates and clothing. Use them as stories to preface your activities on moving.

When Did We Last Move?

Ask children to interview their parents to find out when their last move was. Some children will remember it. Others will have lived in the same place for a long time.

Make a small name tag for each child. Use a map pin to pin it on a map of the United States or world to show where each family last moved from. Some may have been in the same place. A map of the city could show those moves. Connect the present home and the past home with a piece of yarn.

Immigration/Moving

Ask children to interview parents to find out when their ancestors first lived in America. Many will have immigrated. Others will have been here for as long as the family can remember. Place the dates on a time line to show when the family first lived here and the countries from which they immigrated (if they immigrated).

Keep in Touch

As children leave your classroom, send them with self-addressed stamped envelopes and stationery in order that they may write to your class and stay in touch. Memories and letters are lifesavers in some moves. It's a great way for your children to get pen pals.

Mrs. Puckett's Class
Sunnyside Elementary
2114 Palo Verde Rd.
Tucson, AZ   85704

Children's Books

Baines, R. *Harriet Tubman: The Road to Freedom.* U.S.A.: Troll Associates.

Brenner, B. (1978). *Wagon Wheels.* New York: Harper & Row Publishers.

Brown, T. (1991). *Lee Ann: The Story of a Vietnamese-American.* New York: G. P. Putnam's Sons.

Bunting, E. (1988). *How Many Days to America? A Thanksgiving Story.* New York: Clarion Books.

Duarte, M. (1968). *The Legend of the Palm Tree.* New York: Grosset & Dunlap Publishers.

Gray, N. (1988). *A Country Far Away.* New York: Orchard Books.

Hickman, M.W. (1979). *My Friend William Moved Away.* Nashville: Abingdon.

Hoyt, H.P. (1974). *Princess Kaiulani.* Honolulu: Island Heritage Books.

Hughes, S. (1978). *Moving Molly.* Englewood Cliffs, NJ: Prentice-Hall, Inc.

Jones, P. (1980). *I'm Not Moving.* Scarsdale, NY: Bradbury Press.

Krensky, Stephen. (1991). *Children of the Earth and Sky.* New York: Scholastic, Inc.

Levine, E. (1986). *If You Traveled West in a Covered Wagon.* New York: Scholastic, Inc.

McGovern, A. (1969). *If You Sailed on the Mayflower.* New York: Scholastic, Inc.

Sandin, J. (1981). *The Long Way to a New Land.* New York: Harper & Row Publishers.

Surat, M.M. (1983). *Angel Child, Dragon Child.* New York: Scholastic, Inc.

Turner, A. (1985). *Dakota Dugout.* New York: Aladdin Books, Macmillan Publishing Company.

Williams, K.L. (1991). *When Africa Was Home.* New York: Orchard Books.

GA1432

Immigration/Moving
Take-Home Book

Read the story. Color the pictures. Cut out the boxes. Put the story in order. Staple the story together. Make a cover. Read the story to a friend. Take the book home. Read it to someone at home.

We planned a move.

We moved our tables.

We moved our books.

We cleaned our room.

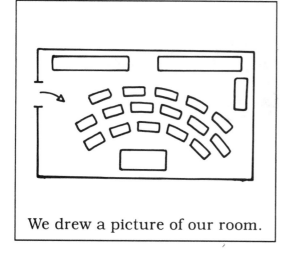

We drew a picture of our room.

We like the way it looks.

Many people move to new places.

82

Moms

As with *dad*, *mom* is a nickname for one's mother. Most parents will realize that the name comes from the first utterances of the baby–mama. The term *mother* is used in a variety of ways–Mother Earth, Mother Goose, Mother Teresa. However, we will be looking at moms as the mothers of the children in your classrooms.

In most early societies the father was the head of the family. The mother took charge of things in the father's absence as he went out to hunt. The wealth was tied up in what the father returned with and so he was in charge. In the Hopi tribes, the ancestory and land is in the maternal line. Today, because of the sharing of financial responsibilities in the families, both moms and dads share the decision making in many families.

Dads and moms play a major role in socializing their children. Since young children learn their social skills from those around them, they are continually influenced by those they are closest to.

Mom's Book

Give each child several small pieces of paper. On each have him draw or write about something his mom does and put his name on the back of each. Let him use as many sheets as he wants. Use these sheets of paper for the following activities.

Share: Take the sheets to circle time. Have each child hold his own sheets in his hands at circle time and share with the others what his mom does, one sheet at a time, around the circle until all sheets have been shown. As each does his one sheet, have him place it on the floor in a pile.

Graph: See if the children can tell you some of the things that lots of moms do and make a list of those on a class graph. Let the children place their sheets of paper in the columns or rows to show how many moms do each of those activities. After the graph has been made, admired, and used as long as you want, redistribute the pictures to the correct children. This will show the similarities and differences for each child.

Sort: Ask the children to sort their own pictures into piles for work, play and home.

Book: Staple the sheets all together and make a Mom's Book for each child to take home. Make a cover using a piece of construction paper to fold over the book. Glue a white or cream oval to the front. Draw a portrait of Mom in the oval.

GA1432

Where Were You Born?

Use the ditto sheet at the end of this unit to have each child work with his mom to determine where the child, the child's mother, the mother's mother, the mother's mother's mother, etc., were born, going back as far as he can using just moms.

When the children bring these back, plot on a world map where all the children's moms are from. This is most easily done by giving each child a different color of construction paper square to attach to the map with Ticky Tac. Comment on the sameness of the locations and the differences of the locations, making no biases in your statements.

Travelin' with Mom

Give each child a piece of construction paper to make a car, station wagon, truck, mini van or bus, whichever way he travels with his mom. Shape the construction paper into a car, cut out windows, and glue on wheels. Cover the windows with plastic wrap. Make a mom face and children faces to show who goes "travelin' with Mom" and put the faces in the windows.

On the back of the car have the child write (or draw) about where he travels with Mom. Hang as mobiles in the room so people can see both sides of the car.

Mom drove us to the museum so that we could see the new dinosaur exhibit. Afterwards we went and had pizza and root beer.
Angie Schraber

Moms at Work, Home and Play

Have each child bring to school something to tell about what his mom does–at work, home, play. When the children bring these to school, set them on the floor and mix them up. At circle time, hold up one thing at a time. Have the children guess what it tells about a mom. When they have guessed many things, have the owner claim it and tell why he brought it. Continue until all have had a turn.

As a follow-up activity have each child draw a picture of what he brought and write about it under the picture. Post on the bulletin board "Moms at Work, Home and Play."

GA1432

Dads, Families and Grandparents

Refer to the sections on Dads (page 34), Families (page 46) and Grandparents (page 66) for other activities that include what the children do with their dads, families or grandparents; what dads, families or grandparents do at work, play, home and away; listing and alphabetizing names of dads, families or grandparents; trips they take with their dads, families or grandparents; ancestors; places of birth. In each case, use any of the activities suggested and change the focus to moms.

It Reminds Me of Mom

Give each child a piece of paper folded into boxes. Determine the number of boxes by the amount of time you have and the level of your children. Provide the children with magazines, scissors and glue. Remember to get magazines that have many different cultural groups represented. Have children cut out pictures from these magazines that remind them of their moms. Label each picture.

Helping Hands: I Help Mom

Have the children trace around their hands in pairs and color them the right color. Each child works with an adult to write on fingers something he does to help his mom.

Helping Hands: Mom Helps Me

Have each child trace around his mother's hand and color it the right color. Each child then works with an adult to record on each finger something that Mom does to help him.

clean
cook
write
bathe

We Help Each Other

Cut out the hands from both of the above activities and glue them onto a piece of paper, connecting the two hands.

Children's Books

Bannon, L. (1961). *The Gift of Hawaii.* Chicago: Albert Whitman & Company.

Feelings, M. (1974). *Jambo Means Hello: Swahili Alphabet Book.* New York: Dial.

Isami, I. (1989). *The Fox's Egg.* Minneapolis: Carolrhoda Books, Inc.

Stanek, M. (1989). *I Speak English for My Mom.* Niles, IL: Albert Whitman & Company.

Surat, M.M. (1983). *Angel Child, Dragon Child.* New York: Scholastic, Inc.

GA1432

All About Moms

Draw a picture of your mom in the picture frame. Beside it write where she was born.

In the next picture frame draw a picture of your mom's mom. Beside it write where she was born.

If you know about your mom's mom's mom, draw a picture on the back of this paper and write beside it where she was born.

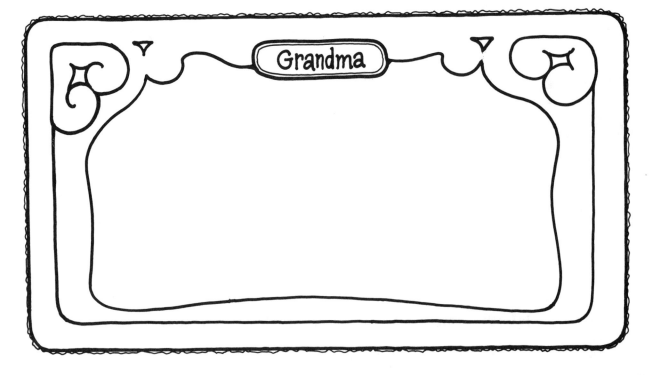

GA1432

Moms Take-Home Book

Read the story. Draw the pictures. Cut out the boxes. Put the pictures in order. Staple them together. Make a cover. Read the story to a friend. Take it home. Read it to someone at home.

My mom

My mom in the morning

My mom at night

My mom at work

My mom is playing.

My mom and me

Different moms do different things.

Names

Your name is perhaps the most important thing about you. Whenever you meet someone new, he generally wants to know what your name is. We have first names, surnames, and nicknames. Some of us have middle names, hyphenated names, maiden names, married names, and confirmation names.

Your surname, which comes from your parents, belongs to you even before you are born. Your personal or given name is bestowed upon you by your family. Later, family and friends often call you by a nickname.

Family names came about in a variety of ways.

1. Some names came from the place where one lived–Brook, Lake, Pond, Pool, Rivers, Du Pont.
2. Some names came from the crafts of the individuals–Coward (cowherd), Smith, Taylor, Weaver, Spinner, Farmer.
3. Some names came from what they had–Coach, Wagon.
4. Some invaders often tacked their words to places they had conquered–Thorp (farm or hamlet) became Winthrop, Calthorp, Wick (village) became Pickwick Greenwich, Wickham.
5. Names ending in *by* come from the Scandinavian word for settlement.
6. Adding the word *son*, *sen* (Denmark and Norway), *nen* (Finland), *ez* (Spain), *ski* (Poland), *mac* (Scotland and Ireland) *ben* (Hebrew) to the name of the father. Adding *O* in Ireland means "grandson."
7. Physical features influenced names. Red, Reid, Reed, or Read in England; Rousseau or Rouse in France; Rossi in Italy; Roth in Germany; Flynn in Ireland.
8. Strength and size gave us the names Little, Small, Power, Strong.
9. Persecution caused people to drop the part of their names indicating group membership. Moses became Moss, Levi became Lee or Low.
10. Conspicuous body parts gave us Brain, Head, Legge.
11. Characteristics like certain animals gave us Fox, Lion, Lamb, Eagle, Falcon.
12. Sources of given names are the Bible, famous people, famous events, personal events.

The spellings of names are a matter of personal choice since many names came about when little was put into writing.

GA1432

What's Your Name?

Names are important to us. Children learn their names and to respond to them very early in life. It is one of the first words they learn to write and read. Give each child a name tag and crayons or markers. Let him write his name on the name tag and decorate. Of course, the teacher and any other adults in the classroom should complete this activity with the children. The finished name tags should be worn during this unit and then taken home.

On a large sheet of construction paper let each child write in pencil his first name. He then can trace over the pencil lines with white glue and sprinkle some substance on the glue that begins with the same sound/letter as his name, e.g. use dirt for David or Deborah, glitter for Glenda or Glenn, brown sugar for Shonda or Shawn, plain white glue for White Feather or Winifred, etc.

Games with Names

Give each child strips of graph paper. Let him write his full name (first, middle, last) on the strips of graph paper putting only one letter in each box and skipping one box between each name. Divide the class into groups of five or six children and ask them to identify the order of each child's name by length. Let each group tape these to the board or wall with the longest name first and continue to the shortest name being last. Next lead them to arrange the whole class in order by the length of the children's names.

The above name strips can now be used to group in piles according to the number of names the children have. Graph the results and discuss why some children may have more names than others, i.e. hyphenated names, confirmation names, family or cultural tradition, etc.

Whose Calling?

Many children have nicknames and or pet names bestowed upon them by family and friends. Some of these names are not known by others. Give each child several pieces of paper and ask him to write on the paper nicknames and pet names that family and friends call him or did call him when he was younger. Only one name should be written on each piece of paper. Each child should select one of the names. Collect the names and mix them up. Choose one name at a time and see if the class can match the nickname or pet name with the correct child or children.

Let the children group the names into piles of matching names and graph the results. What is the most common nickname/pet name in your class?

Ask your children to separate their nicknames/pet names into those names they are still called versus the names they were called when they were younger but are no longer used.

What's in a Nickname?

Many times a nickname is given to shorten someone's given name or the nickname matches some characteristic he has. On a sheet of paper ask each child to write his given name across the top of the paper. Below his name he should draw a picture of himself, and at the bottom of the page write his nickname and how he got the name.

Where Does Your Name Come From?

Ask your students to tell where their names came from (see p. 92). This would include cultural origins, people they are named after, etc. Also ask the librarian for some reference books that list names, meanings, and origins. Chart your children's names by origin and how they got their names.

Name Trends

Give each child as many pieces of paper squares as he has members in his family. This should include himself (manila paper square), parents (yellow paper squares), siblings (light-green paper squares), aunts/uncles (blue paper squares), first cousins (pink paper squares) and grandparents (brown paper squares). Ask him to write on the appropriate color of paper square the given name of each family member. You may need to send a fill-in-the-blank sheet home with each child so that parents can help their child write the given first names of their family members prior to doing this activity in the classroom.

Ask each child to alphabetize the first names of his family members (the paper squares). This will mix the colored paper squares. Now have the children alphabetize all of the names by placing their cards in piles following the order of the alphabet (A, B, C, etc.).

In the front of the room post large sample pieces of the colored squares with the family member categories on the appropriate color of paper, for example, siblings on light green. Look at the trends in first names by graphing the most commonly used first names of the children's grandparents. Then graph the most commonly used first names of parents and aunts/uncles. Finally, graph the most commonly used names of themselves and first cousins. Talk about the differences and likenesses of popular or common first names from the different generations.

Children's Books

Mosel, A. (1968). *Tikki Tikki Tembo*. New York: Henry Holt and Company.
Balet, J. (1965). *Joanjo*. New York: Seymour Lawrence Delacorte Press.

GA1432

Dear Parents:
Please help your child fill out this information to return to school tomorrow.

First Name:
    Reason(s) for choosing this name:

Middle or Second Name:
    Reason(s) for choosing this name:

Other Name or Names:
    Reason(s) for choosing this name or these names:

List each family member that has had each name listed above or a version of the name and his relationship to your child (aunt, grandfather, etc.).

First Name:

Middle Name or Second Name:

Other Names:

Names Take-Home Book

Read the story. Fill in the pictures and words. Cut out the boxes. Put the pictures in order. Staple them together. Make a cover. Read the story to a friend. Take it home. Read it to someone at home.

My name is _____.

This is my family.

My favorite meal is _____.

My favorite treat is _____.

My name means_____.

These are the names of
some of my friends.

Some names are the same. Some names are different.

94

New Year's

New Year's is a holiday celebrated in almost every country. It is usually celebrated on the first day of the calendar year, January 1, in each country. However, it was not always celebrated on January 1. Some Native Americans started the new year when their crops were ready to be harvested. The Jewish New Year occurs between September 6 and October 5. It isn't on the same day each year. The Chinese New Year is always on a day between January 21 and February 19. When a country or culture celebrates New Year's Day is generally based on religious and seasonal events. Modern customs on New Year's Day include visiting friends and relatives, giving gifts, attending religious services, and making noise with guns, horns, bells and other devices.

Clean Slate

Talk to your class about the meaning of resolutions. Lead them to suggest ways they can improve themselves, for example, respecting elders and peers, neater handwriting, not contributing to classroom noise and chaos, etc. Provide each student with a lap-sized chalkboard and have him write two or three resolutions he is going to personally work to achieve. Have him write these in language that indicates the negative form of the resolution. For example, I will stop teasing (student's name) on the playground. Each day let your students put a mark beside each resolution that he has not broken. If the resolution is broken, the tally marks are erased. When the student has gone five days in a row without breaking a resolution, the resolution can be erased.

GA1432

Ring in the New Year

Long ago, people thought that evil spirits walked about on New Year's Eve. Not wanting to get caught, they made lots of noise with guns, bells, firecrackers, noisemakers, noisy parties, sirens, and/or shouting "Happy New Year." Many people wear funny or ornamented hats and clothes on New Year's Eve while they are celebrating. Provide an assortment of newspapers, colored construction paper, and other craft supplies. Let your students create unique party hats and other decorations to attach to their clothes. Also provide noisemakers or supply the materials for them to make their own noisemakers. Decorate the classroom with brightly colored streamers and other decorations. Ask some parents to provide some punch and treats. When the hats, decorations, and noisemakers are ready, have a noisy New Year's Eve party in your classroom.

Father Time

Both the Greeks and the Ecuadorians use the Father Time (old man) figure to represent the old year during their New Year's celebrations. The Greeks were the first country or culture to use the baby to represent the new year. Provide construction paper, scissors, markers or crayons, and pieces of scrap material for your students. Ask them to cut out shapes to represent the baby and Father Time. Markers, crayons, scraps of paper and material can be used to add eyes, hair, clothes, diaper, etc., to the figures. Each figure can be pasted to another sheet of paper, and the two sheets can be connected by a strip of construction paper to represent that each year is connected to each other even though we number them differently.

Flower Pictures

Provide your students with 1"-2" (2.54 x 5.08 cm) squares of tissue paper in a variety of colors, construction paper, scissors, pipe cleaners, markers, and white glue or glue sticks. Some countries, like China, decorate their homes with flowers for New Year's. Let your students use the above materials to make paper flower pictures and paper flowers that can be used to decorate the classroom.

Parades

Read the book *Lion Dancer: Ernie Wan's Chinese New Year* to your students. Talk about the parade and the lion dance. Provide large pieces of butcher paper, paper sacks, large pieces of colored material, crepe paper, tape, scissors, and crayons. Let students look through the book and others that have pictures of the lion and Chinese dragon costumes for ideas. Help them make lion and dragon costumes. Once the costumes are made and they practice how they are going to dance in them, have a parade through the halls and onto the playground.

Celebrations

When students bring back the survey that describes how their families celebrate the New Year's holiday, graph the different ways listed. Let some of the children describe some of the unique customs mentioned and what they mean. Perhaps some of the families that have special foods for their New Year's celebrations would send them to school so that the class might try them. For simple recipes, you could gather the materials and help the children prepare the special foods for their classroom festive party.

Chase the Dragon's Tail

In the book *Games from Many Lands*, a game is described where a leader, followed by children in a line connected by one hand on the shoulder of the person in front of them, tries to catch the last person in line–the tail. When the tail is caught, the leader drops out and the tail becomes the leader. The game is over when there are only two players.

Children's Books

Benarde. A. (1970). *Games from Many Lands*. New York: The Lion Press.

Brown, T. (1991). *Lee Ann: The Story of a Vietnamese-American*. New York: G.P. Putnam's Sons.

Politi, L. (1960). *Moy Moy*. New York: Charles Scribner's Sons.

Waters, K., and Slovenz-Low, M. (1990). *Lion Dancer: Ernie Wan's Chinese New Year*. New York: Scholastic, Inc.

Wyndham, R. (Ed.). (1968). *Chinese Mother Goose Rhymes*. Cleveland: The World Publishing Company.

How Does Your Family Celebrate New Year's?

We are studying how different families and cultures celebrate New Year's. Please help your son or daughter share with us how your family celebrates this holiday. Briefly describe your family's customs and traditions for New Year's.

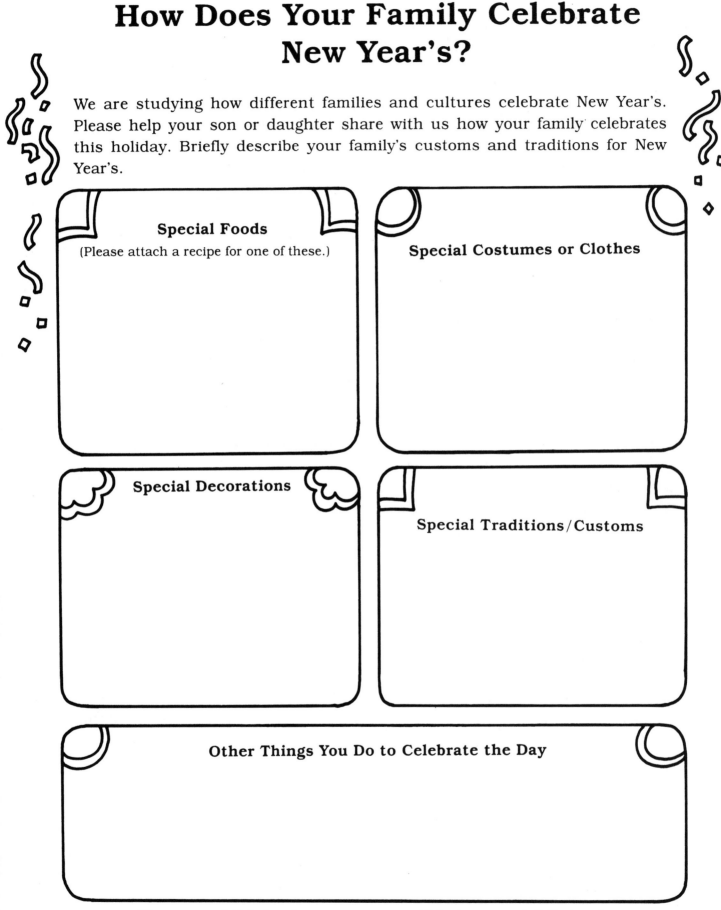

Special Foods

(Please attach a recipe for one of these.)

Special Costumes or Clothes

Special Decorations

Special Traditions/Customs

Other Things You Do to Celebrate the Day

Please send this back as soon as possible to your child's teacher.

GA1432

New Year's Take-Home Book

Read the story. Draw the pictures. Cut out the boxes. Put the pictures in order. Staple them together. Make a cover. Read the story to a friend. Take it home. Read it to someone at home.

This is me on New Year's Eve.

This is my family celebrating.

We celebrate with food.

We celebrate with a party.

We celebrate with noise.

We celebrate.

99

People celebrate New Year's in different ways.

100

Peanuts

Peanuts and peanut products are readily available for use in the classroom at any time of the year. They can be shelled (fine motor), eaten (health), cooked (science), grown (science), counted (math), sung about (music), read about (language), written about (language).

Although George Washington Carver discovered many uses for the peanut, he did not discover the peanut itself. Those Hispanic and Native Americans whose families have roots with the Incas can claim that their ancestors were the first to grow and eat peanuts. Archaeologists have unearthed jars shaped like peanuts that were made by the Inca Indians. The Spanish explorers took them home and then into Africa and Asia. The natives in Africa considered them to be a valuable food source and brought peanuts with them on the slave ships into the Virginia colonies.

Since cotton and tobacco were the leading crops in the south, peanuts were grown only near the slave cabins until after the War Between the States. The soldiers on both sides in this war once again considered them a valuable food source and used the "goober pea" for quick energy. Peanuts should not be considered junk food. They contain more protein than eggs, dairy products and many different kinds of meat. (Information from the Hubbard Peanut Co., Inc., Sedley, VA 23878)

There are several types–Runner, Jumbo and Bunch, all domestically grown. They can be purchased in shell, shelled, candied, glazed, buttered, salted, roasted, meal, peanut butter, honey roasted, etc.

The Mystery Box

Pack a box with many different kinds of peanuts and peanut products. Include peanut butter; nuts in the shell un-roasted; nuts in the shell roasted; shelled nuts; chopped nuts; peanut butter sandwiches in a Ziploc bag, quartered and enough for each child to have one.

Present the box to the children at circle time. Ask a different child to come up, take an item out of the box, and describe it.

Have children eat peanut butter sandwiches while you tell them about how these peanuts got to us, historically and today.

The Travels of the Peanut

While the children nibble on small pieces of peanut butter sandwiches, get a globe and tell the children the historical information that is provided at the beginning of this unit. Tape a string in South America, take the string and tape it to Spain, continue the path to Africa, to Virginia, and then to where you live. Place the globe in the writing center. Children may choose to write about the travels of the peanut, writing the names of the countries and oceans from the globe.

All About Peanuts

Provide each child with several pieces of peanut-shaped paper at least 8" (20.32 cm) in length. On each piece of paper, have him draw one thing from the peanut mystery box, label it, and write what he can about it.

Use a brown/tan peanut-shaped piece of paper to make a book cover. On the back, draw three lines. Have the child take the book home to read to three people. Have the three people sign the back of the book. When it has been signed, have the children return it to school and receive a small bag of peanuts as a prize.

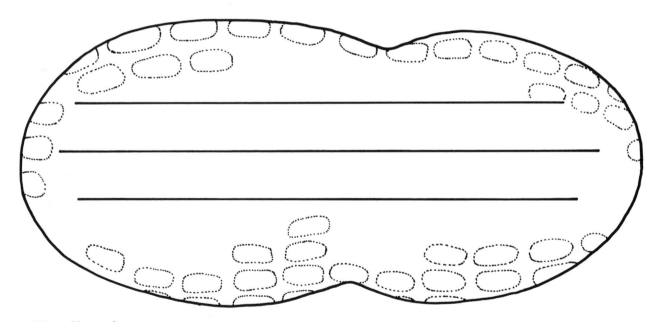

Handiwork

Place peanuts in the shell in a fine motor center with newspapers, bowls, and cups. Demonstrate how the children can shell the nuts, put the shells on the newspaper, and put the nuts in the bowls. When they are ready to eat, they can fill a cup with water and eat their work.

What's in the Shell?

Children can save the shells; fill them with cotton or fake moss; and put miniature animals, birds, eggs in them as decorations.

The Old Man in the Nut

If a shelled peanut is broken in half along the splitting line, there will be a shape at one end of one half of the nut that looks like an old man with a beard.

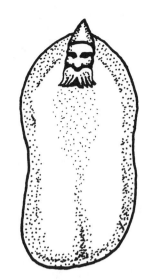

Give each child several shelled nuts and two cups. Have him break the nuts in half and find the man in the nut. Put the nut halves that have men in them into one cup and the halves that don't have men in them into another cup.

When the child is finished, have him count how many men he has and how many halves he has that have no men in them. They should number about the same. Let him compare his numbers with his classmates.

"Found a Peanut"

This old song is one children enjoy and drives adults wild. Teach it to them and let them sing it outside. Modify the old song which says that they ate a rotten peanut, got sick, died, went to heaven. Use the verses below.

Verse One

Found a peanut, found a peanut
Found a peanut just now
Just now I found a peanut,
Found a peanut just now.

Other Verses

Cracked it open, cracked it open
Ate the peanut, ate the peanut
It was yummy, it was yummy
Found another one, found another one
(Return to cracked it open and sing on and on and on and on and on.)

Goober Peas

The chorus to the song is great fun to sing:

Peas, peas, eating goober peas.

Goodness, how delicious, eating goober peas.

For the rest of the words, see the *Wee Sing America* book and tape.

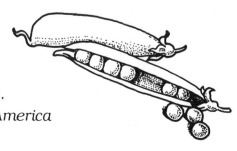

103

Eat Those Peanuts

Try several different peanut butter recipes. Copy. Let the children cut them out and put them in peanut-shaped books for their parents.

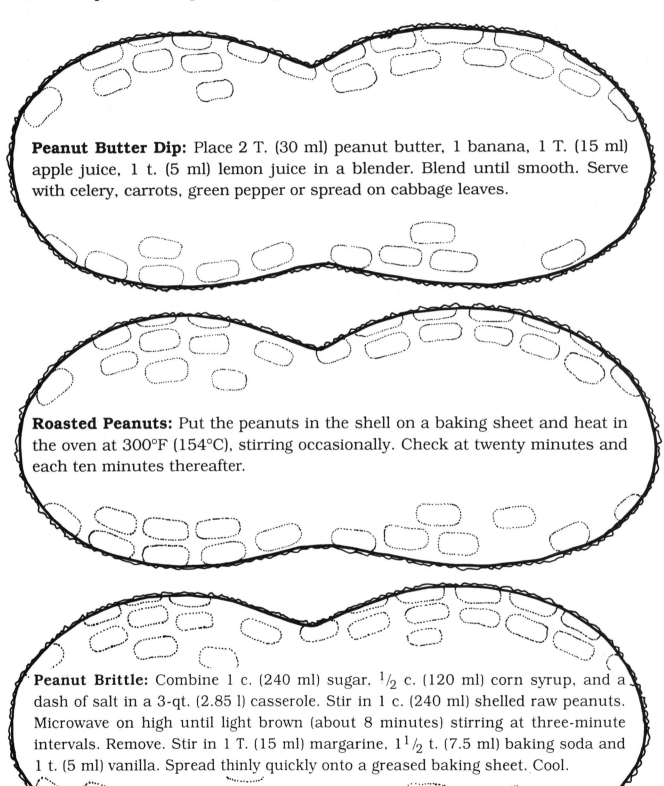

Peanut Butter Dip: Place 2 T. (30 ml) peanut butter, 1 banana, 1 T. (15 ml) apple juice, 1 t. (5 ml) lemon juice in a blender. Blend until smooth. Serve with celery, carrots, green pepper or spread on cabbage leaves.

Roasted Peanuts: Put the peanuts in the shell on a baking sheet and heat in the oven at 300°F (154°C), stirring occasionally. Check at twenty minutes and each ten minutes thereafter.

Peanut Brittle: Combine 1 c. (240 ml) sugar, $\frac{1}{2}$ c. (120 ml) corn syrup, and a dash of salt in a 3-qt. (2.85 l) casserole. Stir in 1 c. (240 ml) shelled raw peanuts. Microwave on high until light brown (about 8 minutes) stirring at three-minute intervals. Remove. Stir in 1 T. (15 ml) margarine, $1\frac{1}{2}$ t. (7.5 ml) baking soda and 1 t. (5 ml) vanilla. Spread thinly quickly onto a greased baking sheet. Cool.

Peanut Butter Sandwiches: Add 1 c. (240 ml) pared, cored and finely chopped apple to 4 T. (20 ml) peanut butter with 1 t. (5 ml) lemon juice. A bit of mayonnaise will make it a smoother consistency. Serve on whole wheat bread.

Peanut Butter Cookies: Mix $\frac{1}{2}$ c. (120 ml) butter flavored Crisco, $\frac{1}{2}$ c. (120 ml) peanut butter, $\frac{1}{2}$ c. (120 ml) sugar, $\frac{1}{2}$ c. (120 ml) brown sugar, 1 egg. Add $1\frac{1}{4}$ c. (300 ml) flour, $\frac{3}{4}$ t. (3.75 ml) soda, $\frac{1}{2}$ t. (2.5 ml) baking powder, $\frac{1}{4}$ t. (1.25 ml) salt and $\frac{1}{2}$ t. (2.5 ml) vanilla. Bake ten to twelve minutes at 375°F (191°C).

Peanut Butter Soup: Saute (don't brown) 2 T. (30 ml) margarine with 1 T. (15 ml) diced onion and $\frac{1}{2}$ c. (120 ml) diced celery for 5 minutes. Add 2 T. (30 ml) flour until smooth. Add 2 c. (480 ml) hot chicken broth and cook for 30 minutes. Remove from heat and strain. Stir in $\frac{1}{2}$ c. (120 ml) peanut butter, a dash of salt and 1 t. (5 ml) lemon juice. Sprinkle with chopped peanuts before serving. (Modified from Hubbard Peanut Co., Inc.)

Peanut Pairs

Materials Needed: several peanuts in the shell

Working Groups: pairs of children

Let the children watch as you shell several peanuts. Hand out the peanut halves to children and ask them to find pairs.

Peanut Prints

Materials Needed: peanut shells, thick paint in flat dishes, paper

Working Groups: individuals at a painting table

Let children fill their papers with the peanut shell prints. They can make the shell shapes into anything they want. Try flowers, trees, exploding circles to the edge of the paper.

Resource Book

Aliki. (1965, 1988). *A Weed Is a Flower: The Life of George Washington Carver.* New York: Simon & Schuster, Inc.

George Washington Carver was a black scientist who was born into slavery in Missouri. As an infant he was stolen from his owners with his mother. His mother died, and he was returned to his owners who raised him until he was ten. His love of plants led to his being named the Plant Doctor.

George wanted to go to school, but most schools did not allow black students. He left home at ten travelling in Missouri and Kansas, living with families who would take him in near schools he could attend. He saved money for college and finally had enough by the age of thirty. Again, he had to move to Iowa to find a college that wanted a black student.

In college he studied agriculture and once again became known as a plant doctor. His teaching and research at Tuskegee Institute in Alabama led the land owners in Alabama to move away from planting only cotton to planting sweet potatoes and peanuts. George Washington Carver discovered over 300 ways to use peanuts.

Discussion Questions

1. Why did people call George Washington Carver a plant doctor?
2. Why do you think his parents named him George Washington Carver?
3. List how many ways you can think of to use peanuts. Count them.
4. What do you have to do to take care of a plant? Of people?

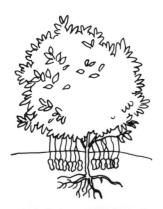

GA1432

Peanuts Take-Home Book

Read the story. Color the pictures. Cut out the boxes. Put the pictures in order. Staple them together. Make a cover. Read the story to a friend. Take it home. Read it to someone at home.

This is a peanut plant.

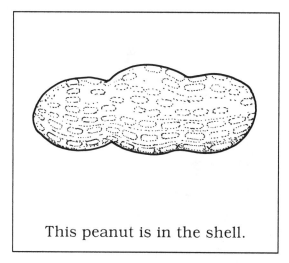

This peanut is in the shell.

This peanut is ready to eat.

This is how I like peanut butter.

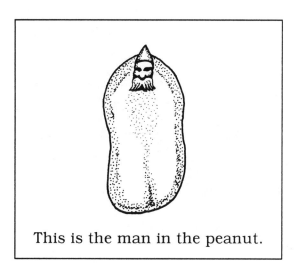

This is the man in the peanut.

This is peanut soup.

There are lots of ways different people eat peanuts.

108

Play

Play has always been an important part of a young child's development. It became a critical part of a child's educational process in the seventeenth century with the thoughts of John Amos Comenius who believed that a positive learning experience for children should include freedom, joy and pleasure.

The National Association for the Education of Young Children has printed *The Developmentally Appropriate Practice Guidelines for Early Childhood Programs Serving Children from Birth Through Age 8*. It is still their position that early childhood programs should provide opportunities for children to freely explore and think about their environments.

It is not easy for us to define *play*. Most theorists would say that it is characterized by attention to a means rather than an end, includes active involvement, is flexible, is pleasurable, spontaneous, and free from externally applied rules. Just what does that mean in the classroom and at home?

It is easier for young children to define *play*. It seems to be about anything that they choose to do and is free from the paper/pencil work of the classroom. Children perceive work to be what an adult tells them to do and things involving the use of pencils.

As you delve into the play habits of children in your room, remember to be accepting of what they say they do in play–they are many times modelling what is happening in their world. They play house. They play war. They play gangs. They play in the sandbox. They play down by the river. They drive cars. They play guns. It is not our position to judge, but to help young children compare and contrast play to formulate just what play is and means to people.

Children at Play

Send home the "At Play" ditto found further in this unit asking parents to make a list, send photographs or draw pictures telling about their child at play. These lists can be used to generate information for the following four activities.

GA1432

Inside Play

Give each child a piece of construction paper to make a house. The body of the house may be square or rectangular–children should choose the shape and color to match their houses. They should adorn the houses with windows, a roof, doors.

Give each child small pieces of white paper. On each piece of white paper have him draw one of the things he worked with his parents to record in the "This is what I do when I play inside" part of the "At Play" ditto. Glue these to the back of the house. On the top of the back of the house, print "At Play Inside."

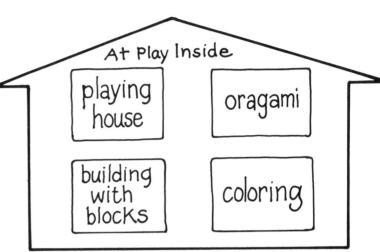

Outside Play

Give the children pieces of 12" x 18" (30.48 x 45.72 cm) paper. Have them make landscapes similar to the one in your area out of construction paper. Grass can be frayed paper, sky with puffy cotton clouds, trees of construction paper and artist tissue paper, sandy areas with sand, dirt areas with dirt, watery areas with cellophane.

When the landscapes are finished, have each child draw a picture on a piece of paper of what he does when he plays outside and write a description at the bottom. Glue onto his landscape.

Outside Play

GA1432

All by Myself

Ask each child to draw a picture of himself on a 6" x 6" (15.24 x 15.24 cm) square playing alone in whatever activity is his most fun activity to play alone. Have him write his name at the bottom of the paper.

When all the pictures are drawn by all the children, have them tell about what they are doing. Record at the bottoms of the pictures what they say. Collect all the pictures. Review them all with the children after each child has had a chance to tell about what he is doing.

Sort the pictures into piles of like activities. See how many different piles you have. Count the number in each pile by placing them in columns. A class graph emerges.

Place the pictures in a center where the children can sort them, compare and contrast them, and count them.

Playing Together

Ask the children to tell you about what it is they like to do when they play with other people, sharing the information from the "At Play" sheet they brought from home.

Group them together with others who like to do the same things.

Give each child a 12" x 18" (30.48 x 45.72 cm) sheet of paper and ask him to draw himself doing what it is that he likes to do with others. Give each group of children who liked to do the same thing a piece of 36" x 36" (.91 x .91 m) paper. Have children cut out individual pictures and glue them on the paper, making the picture show how they play with others.

Playing with Others

111

What Do Others Like to Do When They Play?

Children have looked at what they like to do when they play, and they have seen what their classmates like to do when they play. They have not looked at what younger children like to do and what older children like to do.

If you are in a center where there are younger and older children, suggest that those teachers do this same activity and that you then get together to compare what the different age groups like to do. If not, have children ask little "kids" what they like to do one day, and another day have them ask big "kids" what they like to do. Keep track of the responses and compare them to the class responses.

Examining Play in Children's Books

In each of the books listed below, there is reference to children at play. As you read the books to the children, have them examine the similarities of their play with the children in the book. Ask them to examine the differences. See if they can come up with why there are similarities and differences. In some cases, the materials for the play are not available. In others, they might not have thought about playing in those ways.

Children's Books

Brown, T. (1991). *Lee Ann: The Story of a Vietnamese-American.* New York: G. P. Putnam's Sons.

Cannon, C. (1971). *What I Like to Do.* New York: Coward, McCann & Geoghegan, Inc.

Gray, N. (1988). *A Country Far Away.* New York: Orchard Books.

Havill, J. (1989). *Jamaica Tag-Along.* Boston: Houghton Mifflin Company.

Hughes, S. (1988). *Out and About.* New York: Lothrop, Lee & Shepard Books.

Isadora, R. (1983). *City Seen from A to Z.* New York: Greenwillow Books.

Keats, E.J. (1969). *Goggles.* New York: Young Readers Press, Inc.

Keats, E.J. (1970). *Hi, Cat!* New York: Young Readers Press, Inc.

Krensky, S. (1991). *Children of the Earth and Sky.* New York: Scholastic, Inc.

Martel, C. (1976). *Yagua Days.* New York: The Dial Press.

Mendez, P. (1989). *The Black Snowman.* New York: Scholastic, Inc.

Rylant, C. (1982). *When I Was Young in the Mountains.* New York: E.P. Dutton & Co., Inc.

At Play

Dear Parents:
Make a list, send photographs or draw pictures telling about your child.

This is what I do when I play inside.

This is what I do when I play outside.

This is what I play when I play alone.

This is what I play when I play with others.

GA1432

Play Take-Home Book

Read the story. Color the pictures. Cut out the boxes. Put the pictures in order. Staple them together. Make a cover. Read the story to a friend. Take it home. Read it to someone at home.

Some children play tag.

Some children play soccer.

Some children play marbles.

Some children play at home.

Some children play at school.

Some children play with me.

GA1432

In different countries different children play different games.

115

Potatoes

Potatoes are a readily available classroom material at any time of the year. Potatoes are grown in many parts of the world and are a food source for many groups of people. Because of the association with the Irish, many people assume that they originated in Ireland. That is not true, however.

Those Hispanic Americans whose families came from Bolivia, Chile or Peru can claim that their ancestors were the first to grow and eat potatoes. The Andes Mountains were prime farmland for potatoes. The Spanish and English explorers took them to Europe in the 1500's and the English introduced them to the Irish. Ireland came to claim the potato as its principal crop because it grew so well there.

Potatoes then came back to North America in the 1600's and became a major crop with the Irish immigrants in the early 1700's. Potato production is exceptionally high in Idaho, Washington, Maine, Oregon and California.

What's in a Name?

Materials Needed: all the different types of potatoes that you can find (label each potato), gather stacks of small pieces of paper, pencils and crayons, stapler, construction paper for book covers

Working Group: individuals at a writing center

Show the children the various types of potatoes at circle time. Name each potato. Place the label next to it. When you are finished, place all of the potatoes in a writing center.

At the writing center children examine each potato. Each then draws a picture of it on a piece of paper and labels it. When they have as many as they want, as many as you assign, or have them all, staple the pages together and make a cover for the potato book.

Hot Potato

Materials Needed: several potatoes and music

Working Groups: at least two circles of children

Have children pass a potato around a circle or back and forth in pairs while the music plays. When the music stops the one with the potato is "out." *Out* can only mean that that person changes groups, taking the potato with him, and the game starts again.

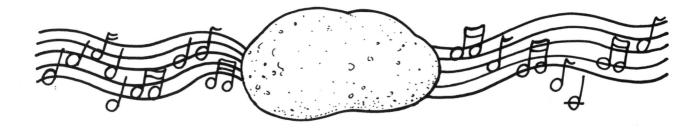

Potato Head

Provide each child with a potato, icing, googly eyes, miniature marshmallows, yarn, scraps of material, soup can, doll clothes.

Each child is to decorate a potato to make a face on it using the materials available. Thick icing will help "glue" the facial features to the potato. When the potato has a face, place it on top of a soup can. Pull the doll clothes up over the top of the soup can and tape them on to stay.

Children can make their potatoes like characters they know or give them names.

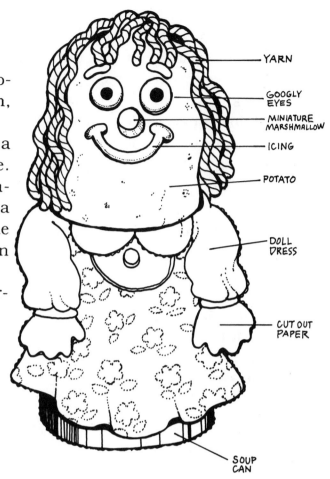

YARN

GOOGLY EYES

MINIATURE MARSHMALLOW

ICING

POTATO

DOLL DRESS

CUT OUT PAPER

SOUP CAN

Potato Pairs

Let the children watch as you cut several potatoes in half. Be sure to cut them so that the halves of each potato are different. Hand out the potato halves to children and ask each to find a partner whose potato half fits his half to make a whole.

To make it more difficult after a couple of times finding matches, cut the halves in half and ask them to group themselves in fours to make the one potato.

Potato Prints

Materials Needed: potato, knife for cutting, pencil for tracing, thick paint in flat dishes, paper

Working Groups: individuals

To make a potato to print with, cut a potato in half. On the flat side place a pattern. Trace around the pattern with a pencil, cutting deep into the potato. Trim away the edges with a sharp knife, making the indentation about $1/2$" (1.25 cm). Let children fill their papers with the potato prints. To investigate different shades of green with the shamrocks, have three dishes of paint, white, yellow and green. Allow children to dip from one to the other.

Eat Those Potatoes!

Materials Needed: potato peelers, potatoes, pans/stove for boiling, condiments (sour cream, chives, dill, butter, ketchup, mustard, mayonnaise, gravy, cheese, bacon chips, and whatever else might go on potatoes)

Working Group: two groups

Children can work in small groups at a center each peeling a potato which is then put into a pot of cold water. When each has peeled one potato, wash potatoes and cut into quarters. Boil until done. Place the potatoes in a large bowl.

Divide children into two groups. One group is the assembly line where potatoes are to be fixed. The other group will be the customers.

Customers tell the first person how large a portion they want and it is dished up.

The assembly line group gets in place, each with an individual task. Each person in the assembly line is responsible for one condiment. The bowl is passed from hand to hand and a simple "yes, please" or "no thank you" will give the "order."

When half of the class has finished, let them eat. They then switch places with the assembly line people.

Children's Books

Watts. *Potato.* Silver Burdett.

Selsam, B. (1972). *More Potatoes!* New York: Harper & Row Publishers.

Hirah, M. (1978). *Potato Pancakes All Around.* Bonim Books.

Goffstein, M.B. (1980). *Laughing Latkes.* Farrar-Straus, Girioux.

Potato Ditto

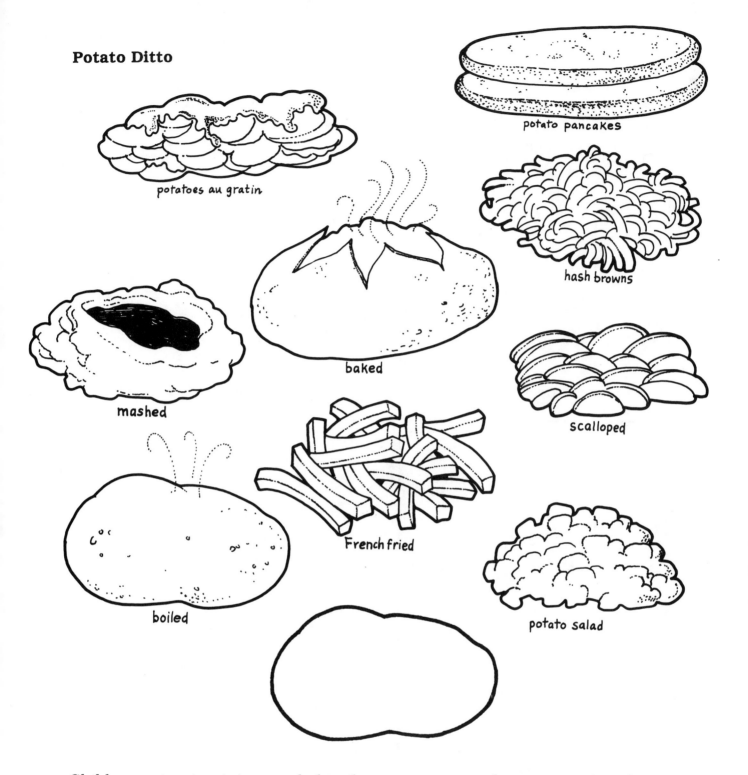

potato pancakes

potatoes au gratin

hash browns

baked

mashed

scalloped

French fried

boiled

potato salad

Children cut out potatoes and glue them onto pieces of paper in order of their preference. They eliminate those they don't know and add their own to blank potatoes.

baked
French fried
boiled
potato salad
mashed potatoes

potato pancakes
hash browns
potatoes au gratin
scalloped potatoes

Potatoes Take-Home Book

Read the story. Color the pictures. Cut out the boxes. Put the pictures in order. Staple them together. Make a cover. Read the story to a friend. Take it home. Read it to someone at home.

These potatoes are baked.

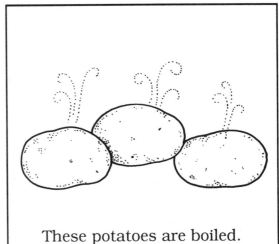

These potatoes are boiled.

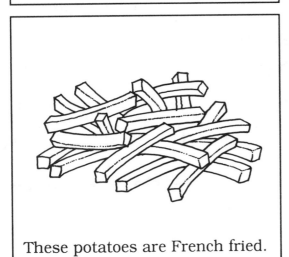

These potatoes are French fried.

These potatoes are scalloped.

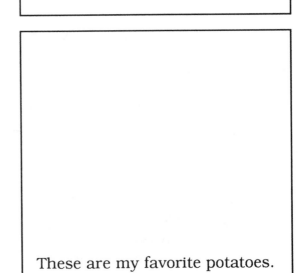

These are potato pancakes.

These are my favorite potatoes.

Different people eat potatoes in different ways.

121

GA1432

Schools

Because families today are increasingly mobile, some of our children are likely to attend more than one school in any one year. In fact, some of them will attend six to ten schools in a year. Still others will stay in the same school from the beginning of school until graduation. Some children are bused for purposes of integration, and others share time between two families and will attend two different schools in any one year. All of these factors can lead to undue stress on children, causing feelings of insecurity, uncertainty, anxiety, apprehension and fear.

Feelings of insecurity caused by switching schools can be eased by helping children realize that in each school there are children, friends, teachers, principals (directors), classrooms, bathrooms, lunchrooms, offices, phones, moms, dads. The purpose of this unit is to help young children make the comparisons and contrasts in schools they know and schools they can become acquainted with through the children's books listed at the end of this section. We will help them understand that schools are places where groups of children congregate to learn, where there are adults to help them learn and to acquire learning skills, and that there are certain traits that are characteristic of all schools.

All About My School

Take a quiet walk around the school, and ask the children to remember what they see. Older children can take along paper and pencil to record three specific things that they see. Younger children can whisper to you what they see and you can record those things next to their names on your master recording sheet.

Teachers should take photographs or slides of things that the children seem to take an interest in and also of some things that the children might miss.

When back in the classroom, discuss what was seen. Illustrate the building on a large sheet of craft paper, and put all the things the children saw around the building.

When the children get back into the room, form a school word bank for them to write about what they saw. Post the words on a school shape.

GA1432

School Mapping

Enlarge a copy of the blueprint of your school to about 2' x 3' (.61 x .91 m). Take photos of each teacher and class, and tape or glue to the appropriate place on the map. Use rubber cement on the laminated map so you can use it again next year. Use the markers at the end of this unit to mark specific places on the map.

After a trip to the gym, have one child locate your room on the map. Have another child locate the gym. Have a third child trace the path to the gym with his/her finger. Have a fourth child trace the path from the gym to your room. Try this for each trip you take.

After children are familiar with mapping, after they return from the trip, show them where you are going on the map and ask them to show you the way to where you showed them they were to be going. Children can work in pairs to explore the building.

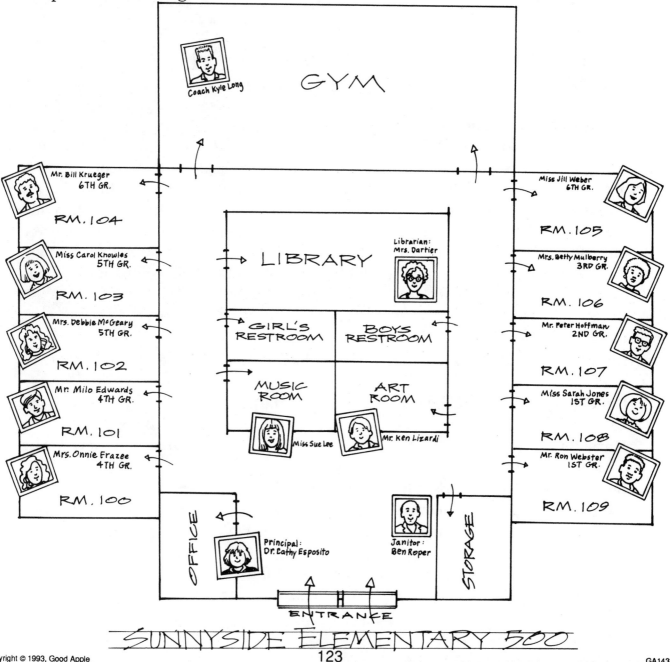

GA1432

Other Schools

Plan a visit to another school, perhaps the school where your children might be bused. Have the children record what they see there, using the same ideas they did with their own school. Introduce children to the teachers and children of their current grade and the next grade. Take slides or photos of your visit from start to finish. Make or copy a map of the new school and mark important areas, the same as you did in your own school. When you get back, note all the similarities and differences in the schools.

Our school	Their school
1. 29,000 sq. ft.	1. 25,000 sq. ft.
2. Yes - we have an art room	2. No art room
3. Our classrooms are smaller	3. Much _bigger_ classrooms
4. GREAT TEACHERS!	4. GREAT TEACHERS!
5. Indoor hallways	5. Outdoor hallways
6. We have _many_ windows.	6. They have very few windows.

Using Children's Books

Each of the books listed below offers a close look at schools in other cities, countries and cultures. All of the children talk about going to school. In most of the books there is something mentioned about what is done in school.

When you read one of the books, make comparisons and contrasts to the children's school and to your own. A fun follow-up activity is to have the children talk with their parents and grandparents about what school was like when they went to school–remember the mile walk to school? Well, elementary school was only one-half mile for me.

Children's Books

Brown, T. (1991). *Lee Ann: The Story of a Vietnamese-American.* New York: G.P. Putnam's Sons.

Lessac, F. (1987). *My Little Island.* New York: Harper Trophy.

Levinson, R. (1988). *Our Home Is the Sea.* New York: E.P. Dutton & Co., Inc.

Margolies, B.A. (1990). *Rehema's Journey: A Visit in Tanzania.* New York: Scholastic, Inc.

Surat, M.M. (1983). *Angel Child, Dragon Child.* New York: Scholastic, Inc.

Waters, K., and Slovenz-Low, M. (1990). *Lion Dancer.* New York: Scholastic, Inc.

Yashima, M., and Yashima, T. (1954). *Plenty to Watch.* New York: The Viking Press.

Yashima, T. (1955). *Crow Boy.* New York: The Viking Press.

Yashima, T. (1958). *Umbrella.* New York: The Viking Press.

Markers

office

classroom

water fountain

bathroom

library

gym

lunchroom

nurse's room

Computer room

teacher's room

parents' room

music room

GA1432

Schools Take-Home Book

Read the story. Color the pictures. Cut out the boxes. Put the pictures in order. Staple them together. Make a cover. Read the story to a friend. Take it home. Read it to someone at home.

Some schools are in homes.

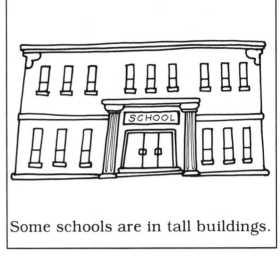

Some schools are in tall buildings.

Some schools are in short buildings.

Some schools are in huts.

Some schools are in churches.

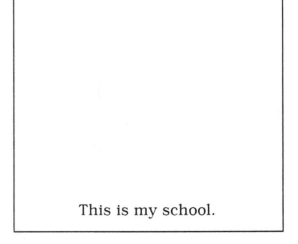

This is my school.

GA1432

Schools can look very different.

GA1432

Shoes

Can you imagine walking barefoot all day long inside and outside, spring, summer, fall, and winter? Hot, cold, wet, dry, smooth, bumpy! Ow! Long ago people got irritated and began making shoes, probably of animal skins or straw tied onto their feet for protective covering. Like clothing, families made shoes by hand and at home for thousands of years until machines were developed, and towns and cities were formed. By 1880 Lyman Blake designed a machine to stitch the soles and upper parts together which speeded up the process. At that point the shoe-making industry took over shoe making. Shoes came to America when the *Mayflower* made its second trip to America.

Shoes were originally made by hand. Pieces of leather were cut with a crescent-shaped knife. The shoemaker then would beat the leather with a lap stone to make it smooth and soft. Holes were punched in the leather with an awl to make sewing easier. For many years the left and right shoes were the same. How uncomfortable. Within the last one hundred seventy-five years two different lasts were used for the right and left shoes.

Shoes were worn for a variety of reasons. Originally they were worn for protection. As time went along, they were often worn for decoration or to communicate a belonging or status to others. Think of what different shoes communicate to you–white saddle shoes, black basketball shoes, sandals, huaraches, cowboy boots, galoshes. Why are these particular shoes worn?

Shoes vary in different countries, in different parts of countries and in different seasons and climates. Check your children's shoes at various times of the year.

Whose Shoes?

Materials Needed: paper to trace shoes on, black crayon, scissors

Working Group: pairs of children

Pair up the children. While one child places his shoes on the piece of paper, have the partner trace around the shoes with a black crayon. Younger children will do better if they trace the sole shape. Older children may turn the shoe on its side and trace it around the whole shoe.

Have children cut out their pairs of shoes and color them to match their own shoes.

GA1432

Pick a Pair

Place all the cutout shoes from the above activity in the center of the circle of children. Let each child pick a pair of shoes and try to find the person they belong to.

Find a Match

Give each child two different shoes from the cutout shoes above. Let him go to the other children to trade a shoe for a match to one of his. As children find pairs, ask them to sit while others finish. While they are sitting, have them try to figure out whose shoes they have.

Pair Them Up

Mix up the cutout shoes from the above activity and put them on a table for children to put into pairs.

Graph the Shoes

Graph the pairs of shoes on a shower curtain graph by color, size or type.

All Kinds of Shoes

Materials Needed: magazines and books, scissors, glue, and long strips of paper

Working Group: pairs of children

Pair up the children and have them go on shoe hunts in magazines, books, and encyclopedias. Choose the books and magazines showing shoes of various cultures and countries.

When children find a pair of shoes, have them cut them out or draw a picture of them and glue them onto a long strip of paper. Let them write or dictate about the person wearing the shoes and name the type of shoes (moccasins, wooden shoes, barefoot, sandals, thongs).

Shoes in a Shoe Box

Materials Needed: shoes in shoe boxes

Working Group: centers for children

Collect several pairs of shoes and shoe boxes. With the children examine how the shoes fit into the boxes. At a center, put all of the shoes in a large box and the shoe boxes nearby. Have the children put the shoes in a shoe box.

GA1432

My Shoes Are Made for Walking (Encouraging Children to Write)

Materials Needed: large piece of storybook (writing) paper for each pair of children, crayons, pencils

Pair up the children. On one half of the paper have them trace around each other's shoes. Title the picture with one of the following:

My shoes are made for walking.
Where do my shoes walk?

My shoes are made for running.
Where do my shoes run?

My shoes are made for climbing.
Where do my shoes climb?

Have children then make a list of all of the places their shoes can take them.

Shoes from Home

Materials Needed: a shoe from home, paper, pencils, and crayons

Ask each child to bring a shoe from home that tells us something about someone at his house. Share the information at circle time. Trace around the shoe on a piece of paper and have the child write or dictate a "story" about the shoe.

What's a Shoe?

Materials Needed: paper, crayons and pencils, shoe word bank

Let each child draw a picture of a shoe and label the parts. Include sole, tongue, heel, toe, arch, laces, eyelets, fastener, buckle, strap.

Children's Books

Clark, A.N. (1979). *In the Land of Small Dragon.* New York: The Viking Press.

Fox, M. (1990). *Shoes from Grandpa.* New York: Orchard Books.

Glasgow, A. (1971). *The Pair of Shoes.* New York: The Dial Press.

Louie, A. (1982). *Yeh-Shen: A Cinderella Story from China.* New York: Philomel Books.

Matsuno, M. (1960). *A Pair of Red Clogs.* Cleveland: William Collins World Publications.

GA1432

In each box draw a picture of one friend's shoes. Write your friend's name on the line in the box.

If you have time, make a box for each person in your class. Cut out the boxes. Put them in a stack. Staple together to make a book. Make a cover page.

GA1432

Shoes Take-Home Book

Read the story. Draw the pictures. Cut out the boxes. Put the pictures in order. Staple them together. Make a cover. Read the story to a friend. Take it home. Read it to someone at home.

These are my shoes.

These are Mom's shoes.

These are my teacher's shoes.

These are Dad's shoes.

These are ball-playing shoes.

These are dancing shoes.

In different places different children wear different shoes.

133

Toys

Children in this day and age have access to many toys, most of which are bought in stores. This has not always been true. The making of toys is a lot like the making of clothes. It was not until the manufacturing machines came into existence that toy making moved out of the home, away from the family and the child himself where he made toys to amuse himself. With the manufacturing of toys, more emphasis is often placed on the commercial value than on the value of play.

A toy should be fun and allow a child to participate with it. It should not have one means, one end. The child will then play with it only once, and it's the end of it. Children can make their own toys, see how they are made, remake them, and replay with them for several days. A purchased playhouse may not be nearly as much fun and take nearly as much imagination as an old refrigerator box which serves for several days as a house, several more as a barn, and several more as a train.

Have children investigate the many ways that toys can be used in order to expand their horizons on the manufactured toys that they bring to share. Try making some toys that they can enjoy both making and playing with.

My Favorite Toy

Send a note home with the children which asks parents to allow the children to bring in their favorite toys for a day. When the children bring the toys, let each one show his toy and tell about it.

Give each child a piece of 4" x 4" (10.16 x 10.16 cm) paper and have him draw a picture of the toy he brought. Use these pictures to classify the toys. Ask the children to tell how the toys might be grouped. Use the groups that they suggest. How many groups did they come up with? Place the pieces of paper in columns to form a picture graph.

Who Makes Toys?

Give each child a piece of paper folded into several boxes. While he has his favorite toy at school, have him examine it and make a list of the words and letters on it, making one word per box. Have him compare his list with a list of one of his classmates. Identify the makers of the different toys and group the toys by makers.

U.S.A	Coleco
Turtle	Singapore

My Mom's/Dad's Favorite Toy

Give each child a piece of paper. Determine how you want him to fold it by the number of parents he will have contact with during the time you allow him to gather the information.

In each box, have the child ask his parents to draw pictures of their favorite toys as children and write a little about them. Have the child bring them back to school to share with his friends. To make them look antique, wet them, wad them up, carefully unfold them and lay them out to dry. When dry, put a frame around it. Frames can be made of construction paper, gold paper, or silver.

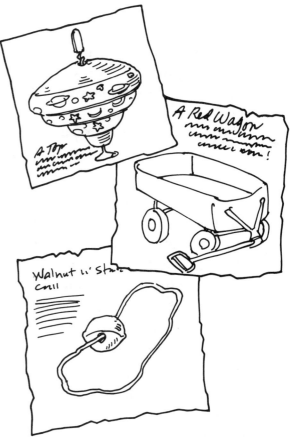

Toys of Others

Children can examine the toys of others when they bring in their favorite toys. If you have many children from different cultures, you may get a variety of toys representative of those cultures. If not, you will need to draw attention to the toys in the list of books on the next page or collect them from various places in the community or largest city near you.

Puppets

Have children make different types of puppets to retell stories that they have read. Toys can be made to become the props in the stories.

Try making finger or pencil puppets. Each child makes a person, colors it, cuts it out and places a strip of paper around the bottom. The strip is then taped around a pencil or a finger. If he places puppets on his pointer and middle fingers, the toy props could then be held with the thumb and fifth finger.

Toy Makers

Place a junk box of materials in an art center. Provide junk such as empty paper towel and toilet paper rolls, tinfoil, wood scraps, buttons, empty spools, plastic spoons, dowel rods of various sizes, plastic margarine containers, lids, string, rope, ribbon, rickrack, season tins. In addition to the junk, have scissors, tape, glue, construction paper, tissue paper, plastic wrap (all colors).

Have the children look at the toys they have brought and the ones in the room and try to make a toy out of the materials in the junk box. Toys can have names, makers, purposes. Short stories and advertisements can be generated by more advanced children.

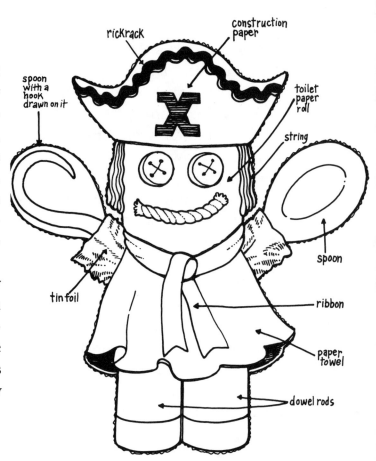

Toys in Books

While you read the children stories for the next several weeks, have them look closely for the toys in the pictures. Talk about whether or not they have toys like them or what they think is done with these toys.

Children's Books

Appiah, S. (1988). *Amoko and Efua Bear*. New York: Macmillan Publishing Company.

Caney, S. (1972). *Toy Book*. New York: Workman Publishing Company.

Cannon, C. (1971). *What I Like to Do*. New York: Coward, McCann & Geoghegan, Inc.

De Paola, T. (1983). *The Legend of the Bluebonnet*. New York: G.P. Putnam's Sons.

Ets, M.H. (1963). *Gilberto and the Wind*. New York: The Viking Press.

Gray, N. (1988). *A Country Far Away*. New York: Orchard Books.

Havill, J. (1986). *Jamaica's Find*. Boston: Houghton Mifflin Company.

Williams, K.L. (1990). *Galimoto*. New York: Mulberry Books.

Williams, K.L. (1991). *When Africa Was Home*. New York: Mulberry Books.

Look at the children in these pictures. Read about them. Draw the toys they need.

These children like to run, jump, yell while they are playing.

These are the toys they need.

These children like to play outside quietly.

These are the toys they need.

These children like to play quietly inside.

These are the toys they need.

Toys Take-Home Book

Read the story. Draw the pictures. Cut out the boxes. Put the pictures in order. Staple them together. Make a cover. Read the story to a friend. Take it home. Read it to someone at home.

These are baby toys.	These are old toys.
These are new toys.	This is a toy box with toys.
This is my newest toy.	This is my favorite toy.

Toys come in all sizes and shapes.

139

The World of Work/Careers

Many people use the term *career* to mean a job, occupation, or vocation. A career involves much more than this. It is the pattern of work and work-related activities that a person develops throughout a lifetime. Almost every adult has a career of some kind. Most careers develop around work for which a person receives pay. However some people build careers around activities for which they receive no pay, for example, creating a comfortable home life for their families, charitable projects, etc.

A career usually affects where a person lives, the friends he makes, how much education he has, how he feels about himself, how other people act towards him, and the amount of money he earns. Knowing one's abilities, interests, and goals will give a person a foundation on which to base career decisions.

Most children begin to form ideas about life and about themselves as individuals during the preschool and elementary years. If they have realistic views of themselves and the world of work, they can be better prepared to make successful career choices.

Who Does What?

Read some stories to your students and ask them to listen for the kinds of work/careers in which each character is engaged. Make a chart on the board or wall with a picture of the characters. Give your students paper, crayons or markers and ask them to draw pictures of one of the characters. Their pictures should include something that tells what kind of career or work they do. Display the pictures on the board or wall chart.

What's My Line?

After students have listened to a number of stories and discussed what kinds of careers/work the characters do, play the game What's My Line. Ask one child to choose a career or type of work. Let the other children ask questions about what kind of work or career he chose. They can ask questions that can be answered only by "yes" or "no." After ten questions (you may want to adjust this number up or down depending on the age level of children you are working with), the class can try to guess what the job/career is that the child has chosen.

GA1432

What Do Your Dad and Mom Do?

Send the Family Career Survey home to be completed by the parent. When the surveys are returned, help the children group similar occupations/jobs together and chart the results on the chalkboard or chart paper. Lead them to see that some jobs require similar skills and fit similar interests. Also compare and contrast the kinds of work done by the grandparents and parents.

Help the children see how the world of work changes over time. Have each student bring something (piece of clothing, tool, etc.) that represents the kind of work his parent(s) does. Let each one tell about the object he brought and the kind of work his father and/or mother does. Be sure that he explains how the object brought is used or related to the kind of work his parent(s) does.

What Will I Be When I Get Bigger?

Provide each student with a piece of construction paper and crayons or markers. Have him fold the construction paper in half and half again. Open the paper up and draw and color the things he likes to do in the top two panels. These pictures might include playing sports, drawing, singing, playing musical instruments, or many other kinds of interests.

In the bottom two panels he should find pictures that represent the kind of work he might like to do when he gets bigger. These pictures could come from newspapers, old magazines, and old books that you provide.

141

GA1432

Let's Pretend

Ask the students to think about all the careers that you have studied so far. Provide them with books and pictures of different kinds of occupations. Let each one choose a job to act out for the class. After each performance let the class try to guess what job/work was acted out.

What's Your Career?

Invite parents or other adults to your class to talk about their work. The speakers should be prepared to tell your students about their careers, how they got interested in them, what they do in a typical day, what they especially like and don't like about the work, what kind of clothing they wear on the job, and what kinds of tools they use. Save time at the end for questions. Write thank-you letters, specifically addressing each career.

Children's Books

Balet, J. (1965). *Joanjo.* New York: Seymour Lawrence Delacorte Press.

Bang, M. (1983). *Dawn.* New York: William Morrow & Company.

Blacker, T., and Winn, C. (1987). *If I Could Work.* New York: Lippincott.

Clark, A.N. (1941, 1969). *In My Mother's House.* New York: The Viking Press.

Florian, D. (1983). *People Working.* New York: Crowell.

Greene, C. (1983). *Mother Teresa: Friend of the Friendless.* Chicago: Children's Press.

Hoyt-Goldsmith, D. (1991). *Pueblo Storyteller.* New York: Holiday House.

Isadora, R. (1983). *City Seen from A to Z.* New York: Greenwillow Books.

Jacobsen, K. (1982). *Mexico (A New True Book).* Chicago: Children's Press.

Krensky, S. (1991). *Children of the Earth and Sky.* New York: Scholastic, Inc.

Lessac, F. (1987). *My Little Island.* New York: Harper Trophy.

Levinson, R. (1988). *Our Home Is the Sea.* New York: E.P. Dutton & Co., Inc.

Martel, C. (1976). *Yagua Days.* New York: The Dial Press.

Martin, P.M. (1968). *Kumi and the Pearl.* New York: G.P. Putnam's Sons.

McNeer, M., and Ward, L. (1954). *Little Baptiste.* Boston: Houghton Mifflin Company.

Merriam, E. (1961). *Mommies at Work.* New York: Knopf.

Politi, L. (1948). *Juanita.* New York: Charles Scribner's Sons.

Oxenbury, H. (1981). *Working.* New York: Simon and Schuster.

Politi, L. (1960). *Moy Moy.* New York: Charles Scribner's Sons.

Scarry, R. (1968). *What Do People Do All Day?* New York: Random House.

Todd, B. (1972). *Juan Patricio.* New York: G.P. Putnam's Sons.

Yashima, M., and Yashima, T. (1954). *Plenty to Watch.* New York: The Viking Press.

GA1432

 # Family Career Survey

Dear Parents:

We are studying The World of Work/Careers at school. Please help your child complete this survey and send it back to school with your son or daughter this week. You may include information about one or both parents.

	Grandparents	Parents
Name of career/occupation:		
How much education/training was required for this work?		
What kind of skills are required to do this kind of work?		
What do you like about this kind of work?		
What kind of clothing is required by this occupation?		
What kinds of tools are used on this job?		

GA1432

The World of Work/Careers
Take-Home Book

Read the story. Draw the pictures. Cut out the boxes. Put the pictures in order. Staple them together. Make a cover. Read the story to a friend. Take it home. Read it to someone at home.

This is me.

This is one thing I like to do.

I also like to do this.

My dad has this career.

My mom has this career.

This is what I want to be when I get bigger.

Different people have different careers.

GA1432

Working Together

Young children do not easily work together on projects. In a safe environment, they need opportunities to explore working together and solving problems. Some children will be better able to do this than others, depending on the types of experiences they have had with other people, children and adults included. Good social skills are learned through modelling rather than direct teaching. (The same is true for "bad" social skills.) What you do in the classroom as you work with the children or other adults will be picked up by the children.

Some things you might examine as you work with adults and children in the classroom include the following:

Use your manners. Ask nicely for things. Say "thank you" when you receive.

Offer to help with the cleanup process.

Work with another person in the activities that are presented.

Verbalize how much easier it is when tasks are accomplished by working together.

Give positive remarks to those students who offer help to others, to work with others to solve problems, who offer support and encouragement to others.

In addition, "cooperative learning is a teaching strategy that involves children of all performance levels working together in small groups to reach a common goal. The process used in reaching the goal may be the most valuable element to the child's development of social skills and academic skills. . . . Cooperative learning creates opportunities for the exchange of more and better ideas rather than working alone or competitively. All subject areas and grade levels can be taught using this strategy. . . . Research suggests that children working together in small groups develop higher self-esteem, a greater concern for others and higher academic achievement." Carroll, J.A., and Seaton, M. (1992). *Cooperative Learning Throughout the Year: Helping Young Children Work Together*. Carthage, IL: Good Apple, pp. 1-2.

Working Together as Partners

Have each child choose a partner for a day, or assign the children to work in pairs for the day.

When they are introduced to the Working Together as Partners activity, tell them that they will work and play with their partner for the whole day or half day. Begin with free time. Ask them to sit to decide what it is they would like to do and how they can do what each one of them wants to do. Your role today will be to observe and intervene whenever necessary to help the children solve problems.

Working Together Bulletin Board

Whatever the season, have the children work together to make a bulletin board. If it is in the fall, give each pair of children a large piece of paper and a set of markers, chalk, or paints. Their task is to work together to make one large tree on their paper to put on the bulletin board. (Other seasons invite Christmas trees, jack-o'-lanterns, snowmen, valentines, leprechauns, flowers, etc.)

When the tree is finished, provide scissors for them to cut it out. Add names to the tree trunk, and pin to the bulletin board.

Who gets to take it home? Can the children decide? Are there other activities the partners do so they can split the products to take home?

Working Together with Playdough

Give each pair of children a large clump of playdough. Ask each pair to make one large statue of a person. Before they begin, see if they can decide how they will proceed with the work and then begin the actual work. Some may choose to divide the tasks, some may work together on separate tasks, some may decide to assign responsibilities to each other or to themselves.

When the statues are complete, have the pair of children tell the others about their statue. Record their responses on a sheet of paper. Stand the statues on a table for display. Tape the recorded responses to toilet paper rolls to make them stand up near the statues.

147

Working Together to Make Tall Towers

Give each pair of children a set of building materials and ask them to work with their partners to try to make the tallest tower that they can make.

Measure the towers. Draw pictures of the towers. Describe the towers. Tear the towers down.

Group two pairs of children together and ask them to make the tallest tower that they can make.

Measure the towers. Draw pictures of the towers. Describe the towers. Tear the towers down.

Read the story *Barrels to the Moon.* Have the children compare that story to the activity that they have just completed.

Cooperative Learning Activities

For a variety of cooperative learning activities specifically designed for use in classrooms with young children, see two recent Good Apple publications, *Cooperative Learning Throughout the Year* and *Cooperative Learning Throughout the Curriculum*. Activities are varied and include working groups of paired instruction, small groups, jigsaw (experts teaching others), and assembly lines.

Children's Books

Bains, R. *Harriet Tubman: The Road to Freedom.* U.S.A.: Troll Associates.

Berson, H. (1982). *Barrels to the Moon.* New York: Coward, McCann & Geoghegan, Inc.

Brown, M. (1947). *Stone Soup.* New York: Charles Scribner's Sons.

Havill, J. (1989). *Jamaica Tag-Along.* Boston: Houghton Mifflin Company.

Mahy, M. 1990). *The Seven Chinese Brothers.* New York: Scholastic, Inc.

McDermott, G. (1972). *Anansi the Spider: A Tale from the Ashanti.* New York: Holt, Rinehart and Winston.

Ortiz, S. (1977, 1988). *The People Shall Continue.* San Francisco, CA: Children's Book Press.

Working Together Take-Home Book

Read the story. Draw the pictures. Cut out the boxes. Put the pictures in order. Staple them together. Make a cover. Read the story to a friend. Take it home. Read it to someone at home.

I can work on coloring with _____.

I work in blocks with _____.

I work together with Mom.

I work together with Dad.

I work together with my teacher.

I work together with my best friend.

GA1432

I can work together with many friends.

150

GA1432